Discovering God

Discovering God

Exploring the Possibilities of Faith

DENNIS McCALLUM

NEW PARADIGM

NEW PARADIGM PUBLISHING

International Standard Book Number 978-0-9836681-3-8

NEW PARADIGM

New Paradigm Publishing
Columbus, OH

Printed in the United States of America

Contents

CHAPTER 1

The Stakes are High

I MAGINE YOURSELF being ushered into a large party room with numerous booths and pavilions, each offering different activities or
products. You can do anything you want at this party. Thousands
of people are busily moving from one booth to another, engaging
in various pursuits. Some booths offer art and music lessons. One
popular section offers assorted sexual experiences. Another offers
drug experiences. A very large booth offers exercises that enhance
people's bodies. Another offers tasks that entitle the participants to be
rich. Yet another booth is a laboratory for scientific research.

One problem: You were just told that you have a viral infection
that will kill you in three hours, if not sooner. The same is true for
everyone else at the party. At this party, everyone dies within three
hours of the time they arrive.

How do you enjoy that party?

All the pieces for enjoyment are there, but the overhanging death
sentence puts a terrible chill on anything you do.

To make matters worse, as you visit various booths you see a
number of people suddenly collapse in sickness and die. Guards carry
them out to be buried. Before long you notice you're feeling sick!

This depressing party might be a sadly true picture of what we face in life. Our span of time might be seventy years instead of three hours, but the effect would be the same. Compressing the time span into three hours only makes it easier to see the problem. Beings that appear and disappear are pointless beings, and if they are conscious beings who know what's happening, they are necessarily unhappy on some level.

Don't fall for the thought that you could help others. Under this picture, they're in the same place you are. They, too, will soon disappear and never remember they were here. You can't side-step this central question—whether life has a purpose. I want to suggest that all formulas for how life might be meaningful, even if we are just a grain of sand on the shoreline of history and will soon be consumed in the solar explosion headed our way, are drivel and nonsense. We should have the courage to face the truth.

The big questions

Are we alone? Are we curious organisms without purpose in a vast universe that doesn't know we're here?

Or are we prefigured, known, perhaps even loved by some great creator?

What is our fate? Are we destined to a non-existence so profound that we won't know we ever existed? Or can we look forward to an awesome future that goes on forever? Is spirituality just something people fabricate because they need it—mere wishful thinking? Or is our sense that we are spiritual beings with deep significance correct?

Perhaps most important: Can we ever really know the answers to questions like these?

Yes, we can, and with a high level of confidence! Not only that, but the news is good—maybe better than you ever would have guessed.

Why not devote some minutes of your life (actually, a few hours) to find out how we can know? If you do, you'll never regret the time you invested.

Matter and the non-material

I watched an icicle drop off my gutter. Is that a significant event, a meaningful event, or just some matter reacting to physical law? I think we know the answer. But am I any different? Am I matter and energy reacting to physical law, or is there more? Why does it seem like I have a consciousness, a self that goes beyond the strictly physical? If I start thinking I have a spiritual side, I am already thinking outside the natural, into the supernatural. Especially if I begin thinking I'm a being that might survive death, I'm thinking of a non-physical dimension. Where would that come from? Quickly, I realize I'm thinking about God.

What if a real God exists—especially if he is someone you could come to know?

Back at the party, as you are wandering from booth to booth, you hear someone trying to get your attention. Looking over, you see a man standing by the corner of a booth gesturing for you to come over. You walk over and ask what he wants. He says, "We've found a door here that the others don't even know about! You can walk out of this door and receive a cure that enables you to live forever! You can even return to the party and enjoy it without the symptoms you've been experiencing."

Obviously, such a claim would be suspicious. It might be a trick. It certainly seems too good to be true. Yet, while caution makes sense, why not go see what he has? You're not going to jump into something for no reason—you want to see evidence that this 'door' thing is authentic. But under the circumstances, it would be unthinkable to walk away without even checking it out. The possibility that the door could offer a cure would be too important to ignore. This book is about such a door: A door to health in this life and a door to life after death. Jesus Christ said, "I am the door; if anyone enters through me, he shall be rescued" (John 10:9).

We're going to look at a dozen or so reasons for thinking God is there and can be experienced. If these reasons carry weight in your mind, it would make sense to call out to God, asking him to reveal himself to you. You wouldn't be committing yourself to anything. You're just saying that if God is real and personal, and especially if it's true that he loves people and wants a relationship with us, he could hear you calling and might answer.

That's what I did. When I reached a point in my life where I began to think my atheism might be mistaken after all, that all my arguments against God could be wrong, I knew I wouldn't be able to rest easy unless I called out to God. It felt pretty weird. I had never prayed in my life, other than doing what I was told as a child. I didn't speak out loud. I just said in my mind, "If you are there, if you hear me, I'm ready to hear back. But I can't just decide to believe; I need something. I need you to show me this is actually real..." and it went on a bit in that direction. I even said I would keep my eyes open and look around for evidence. That seemed fair. Nothing much happened at that moment, but I felt good about it. I felt I had done the right thing. I wasn't going to lie to myself. Then I went to sleep.

I think that's a good starting point for this study. Complete open mindedness includes openness to God.

CHAPTER 2

Ways of Knowing

How can we know real answers to the big questions? We have more than one way.

Making sense

To believe something, it needs to make sense. We are reasonable creatures. Every time we argue something, we use our reason. When we notice two plus two is four, we use reason. When we discern hypocrisy or foolishness we use reason. When we refuse to believe something that is self-contradictory, we use reason. Only a fool would entrust his life to something that is nonsense.

Faith can either be reasonable or blind. Consider the difference in this scenario:

> I go to the doctor because I feel sick. He checks me over, does a blood test and whatnot, before concluding that I have strep throat. He writes out a prescription and says, "This is what you need. You'll feel better in a day or two."

As I walk into the pharmacy, I could wonder if the doctor is correct in this diagnosis and prescription. He could be mistaken. I don't have any certain way to know his diagnosis is correct or that he has prescribed the right medicine, especially because I can't read his writing. What if he's wrong?

On the other hand, he is a doctor. He has many years of training in medicine. I know the government controls who can practice medicine. Then there was that blood test... All things considered, I decide to get the medicine and take it.

That's reasonable faith. I'm still exerting faith in my doctor and his prescription, but how different it would be than this scenario:

I stop by my buddy's house and tell him how I feel. He says, "Come back here; I think I have something for you." In his medicine cabinet, he fumbles through dozens of pill bottles, finally producing one. "Here, you should take this," he offers.

I look at the bottle with some unrecognizable name. "Why do you think I should take this and what is it?" I scowl.

"I don't know," he shrugs. "I think it could be good... I think I took that awhile back and it seemed to work for me."

Would you nod and start popping those pills? Only if you're a fool! Those pills could be anything. You have no reason to believe this is a medicine useful for your condition. Taking these pills would be blind faith—faith without any reasonable basis. It's nothing like the reasonable faith in the previous scenario with the doctor.

As ridiculous as this second story might seem, some people see faith this way. Faith is just something you choose to believe, something you entrust yourself to; but reason has nothing to do with it. That's not the kind of faith we are going to consider in this book. To the contrary, we will assume that if a creator God is real, he must have made us as reasonable, thinking beings. Therefore, whatever we believe had better have a strong basis. This area is too important to fling ourselves out into black space on the theory that something good might happen. Besides, as we'll see, God has gone out of his way to give people powerful reasons to trust him.

Experience

I believe my wife is real. I might not be able to prove it to you but, nevertheless, I'm satisfied with the evidence I have. That evidence includes reason—I could make a good reasonable case for her existence in the real world. But I have more than that to go on. My experience of her is very persuasive to me. In fact, I doubt anyone could convince me she isn't real.

Direct experience matters. When you think about it, everything we see, feel, taste, smell, or hear is a matter of experience. Philosophers have questioned whether the data of our senses can be trusted. So have believers in some eastern religions who think this world is an illusion, and ultimately unreal.

But that's not what I think. I think we're actually here and I think my wife is real. I'm sure of it. If I thought this world is nothing but a dream in the mind of Vishnu (as Hinduism teaches), thinking would be a waste of time anyway. Nothing here would be real.

In fact, we intuitively know we're here, and we can't deny it anyway—who would be doing the denying? So all of us show by our actions and words that we believe our experiences are real. Any conclusions we reach about anything have some basis in our experience, even if it's the experience of reading something on a page.

Interestingly, we can't prove that our senses are telling us the truth about the world. That is a faith position. Proof is simply not possible for what thinkers call our "first principles." The fact is, you have to start somewhere, and your starting point requires faith. Of course, in the case of our senses telling us something real, we have considerable evidence—experience really—to back up our faith.

Combining reason, experience, and faith

So, if reason and experience are both valid ways of knowing, how do they relate to the question of faith?

Faith is when we trust our experiences or reasons enough to act on them.

Suppose I walk into my kitchen, looking for the peanut butter. I look around at the cabinets, but can't remember where I put it. Looking around at the choices, my eyes go to one cupboard; I doubt it would be in there with the pots and pans. Looking at another, I realize it probably wouldn't be there with the dishes, or under the sink. My eyes land on one cupboard to the left of the sink. *It's probably in there,* I think to myself. *That's where I usually put things like that.* So I feel it's reasonable to check that cupboard first, because of previous behavior.

I don't *know* it's in there. I can't *prove* it's in there. But how much evidence do I need in order to walk over and open the door? Walking over to open the cupboard door would be an act of faith; in this case, a low-risk action based on my sense that it's probably the best choice—just like taking my doctor's prescription.

If I do that, and see the peanut butter right there on the shelf, I now can add the evidence of my experience to my earlier reasoning. I now have a combination of reason and experience, resulting in a high level of certainty—just like I can have with God. With God too, I don't need proof or certainty before I exercise faith. I do need a reasonable basis—some level of plausibility that causes taking a step of faith to make sense. Then, if I have a real encounter with God, I will know he is there after all.

Part of my willingness to take action on the peanut butter is the low risk involved. If the jar isn't there, I'll probably just try a different cupboard. Another factor is the desirability: I want my peanut butter! Both of these factors also come into play in one's willingness to take steps of faith toward God. We're not risking much by taking a step toward God and the desirability is high. If God isn't real, nothing will happen.

CHAPTER 3

The Problem of
Verification

We are first going to look at how God has revealed himself through the Bible and how he even provided a way for us to authenticate his revelation. Later, we'll consider other religions as well.

When looking into the Bible, we have an amazing story, woven over a fifteen hundred year period. Dozens of authors contributed books or sections to this collection, but all of them claimed that the words they wrote came from God—that in a real way, God was the ultimate author of the whole collection.[1] They all claimed they were working as part of a larger plan: it was God's rescue plan for the

---

1   These very numerous claims are spread throughout the Bible. As Peter explains, "Above all, you must realize that no prophecy in Scripture ever came from the prophet's own understanding, or from human initiative. No, those prophets were moved by the Holy Spirit, and they spoke from God" (2 Peter 1:20,21). The apostle Paul said, "All Scripture is inspired by God and is useful to teach us what is true" (2 Timothy 3:16). Both Old and New Testament authors were fully aware that their writings were not like other books, but came from God.

world. At the center of this plan was the most shocking part—that God was coming to earth in person to solve the problem between himself and humans!

So the truth claims in the Bible are quite extreme, and if correct, would call for a complete rethinking of everything spiritual. At the bottom line, this book claims that any person can have eternal life and a personal relationship with God, and it's free of charge. The whole bill has already been paid by Jesus. We will examine this whole scenario in more detail later. First, the question is, how could anyone know if such claims were true?

The Bible is unique in the world because it anticipates and answers this need for confirmation.

God's method of self-authentication

If you were God and you wanted to offer humankind evidence that you existed and that people could reach you through a certain source, how would you do it? How would you distinguish your message from other false messages?

For God to authenticate himself, the evidence would have to be readily available to anyone interested. We would not expect it to be hidden or secret. If it is true that God faces spiritual opposition, we would expect that opposition to either counterfeit or try to discredit any message from God. Therefore, God's self-authentication would have to be something unique—something that no one but God could do. It would have to stand up under even the closest scrutiny.

Such self-authentication would be difficult to create.

People usually think of a miracle—a supernatural event—as proof of the presence and working of God, but there are problems with this kind of verification. Suppose God had one of his servants heal someone. We might still doubt. Perhaps the person wasn't really healed. Maybe the person didn't actually have the condition from which he was supposedly healed. Even if the person was healed, can't others do the same thing? It certainly wouldn't be good enough to have such a healing reported secondhand. We hear such miracle stories from every imaginable religious group and they are usually not true.

The same goes for other miracles. If a spokesperson for God rose up bodily into the air, we would have to point out that magicians float their subjects in the air and pass hoops over them all the time. I personally don't know how they do this, but I still don't believe it's a miracle. The same would go for burning bushes, walking on water, and other events that could be simple magicians' tricks.

Suppose a column of fire appeared and a deep and powerful voice spoke out, "I am the Lord." This would certainly be impressive! However, it has problems from God's point of view. How often would he have to stage such an event? Would it be reasonable to think of God making these appearances for every person on earth? If so, it would require no faith at all to follow him. On the other hand, unless he did repeat it for everyone, we would be left with the secondhand reports of others, which wouldn't be convincing.

Even if God personally appeared like this before every person, problems remain. After seeing such an event, I think my first response would be: "Let's see that again!" Besides, even if we admit the event was a supernatural one, how would we know it came from the Creator God himself? Couldn't this event involve an entity other than the God of the Bible? Somehow the authentication has to be linked to the message God wants to send.

In fact, it's not easy to see how God could reveal a message about himself and somehow mark it as uniquely from him. This problem of self-authentication is thorny. No wonder most holy books make no effort at independent confirmation of their message and simply expect people to believe.

A surprising solution

When we turn to the Bible, we find a surprising and satisfying response to the question of verification. The Old Testament book of

Isaiah says God spoke through a prophet to indicate his displeasure that many Israelites were turning away from him, and toward nature deities. To set himself apart from other so-called deities, God said:

> I am the Lord; that is my name! I will not give my glory to another or my praise to idols. See, the former things have taken place, and new things I declare; before they spring into being I announce them to you (Isaiah 42:8-9).

So God is saying that he, as the only real God and the only being in the universe with true omniscience, will demonstrate that he is the one talking. He will do so by declaring, in advance, what the course of future history will hold.

This could be the answer to the problem of verification. If only God knows what the future course of history holds, this could mark such writing as being from him. God challenged Israel's 'gods' to do the same:

> "Present the case for your idols," says the Lord. "Let them show what they can do," says the King of Israel. "Let them try to tell us what happened long ago so that we may consider the evidence. Or let them tell us what the future holds, so we can know what's going to happen. Yes, tell us what will occur in the days ahead. Then we will know you are gods." (Isaiah 41:21-24).

According to this passage, if these gods could declare the course of history before it happens, it would prove they were deities. The ability to foretell events would require one of two things: either the power to cause history to unfold a certain way or the ability to somehow step outside the constraints of time. Either of these would indicate an all knowing and/or all powerful being.

Of course, not all predictions of the future would require divine insight. A general prediction, like "something bad is going to happen tomorrow," or a commonplace prediction, like "my wife will die someday," would prove nothing. On the other hand, only God can describe detailed, unusual events far into the future, according to these passages. It therefore fits one of the key requirements we saw earlier: the verifying act cannot be done by anyone other than God.

In order to guarantee authenticity, the predictions would have to be set down in writing and the written material would have to be reliably dated before the events described. Also, the predictions should be detailed and extraordinary enough to make coincidence implausible.

The Bible repeatedly stresses God's unique ability to tell the future as a defining mark of supernatural power and insight found nowhere else.[2] This concept of verification through prediction is not new in Isaiah. All the way back in Deuteronomy (1400 BC) Moses had set forward the same test as a way to know true prophets from false ones.

> But you may wonder, "How will we know whether or not a prophecy is from the Lord?" If the prophet speaks in the Lord's

---

2   Here are some more examples from Isaiah:

Thus says the Lord, the King of Israel and his Redeemer, the Lord of hosts: "I am the first and I am the last, and there is no God besides Me. Who is like Me? Let him proclaim and declare it; Yes, let him recount it to Me in order, from the time that I established the ancient nation. And let them declare to them the things that are coming and the events that are going to take place. Do not tremble and do not be afraid; Have I not long since announced it to you and declared it? And you are My witnesses. Is there any God besides Me, Or is there any other Rock? I know of none" (Isaiah 44:6-8)

"Ignorant are those who carry about idols of wood, who pray to gods that cannot save. Declare what is to be, present it—let them take counsel together. Who foretold this long ago, who declared it from the distant past? Was it not I, the Lord? And there is no God apart from me, a righteous God and a Savior; there is none but me. Turn to me and be saved, all you ends of the earth; for I am God, and there is no other" (Isaiah 45:20-22).

"I am God, and there is no other; I am God, and there is none like me. I make known the end from the beginning, from ancient times, what is still to come. I say: My purpose will stand, and I will do all that I please" (Isaiah 46:9-10).

"Long ago I told you what was going to happen. Then suddenly I took action, and all my predictions came true. For I know how stubborn and obstinate you are... That is why I told you what would happen; I told you beforehand what I was going to do. Then you could never say, 'My idols did it. My wooden image and metal god commanded it to happen!'" (Isaiah 48:3-7).

name but his prediction does not happen or come true, you will know that the Lord did not give that message (Deuteronomy 18:21, 22).

Obviously, God would not make mistakes when predicting the future. He wouldn't be guessing, but would know with certainty what is coming.

The New Testament

Jesus also regularly pointed to fulfilled predictive prophecy as the proof of his own authenticity. For instance, in Luke 24 Jesus pointed to the predictions of his actions in the Old Testament as the evidence that he was the savior of humankind.[3] He said to his followers:

> This is what I told you while I was still with you: Everything must be fulfilled that is written about me in the Law of Moses, the Prophets and the Psalms." Then he opened their minds so they could understand the Scriptures. He told them, "This is what is written: The Christ will suffer and rise from the dead on the third day, and repentance and forgiveness of sins will be preached in his name to all nations, beginning at Jerusalem. You are witnesses of these things (Luke 24:44-48).

The other writers of the New Testament also argued that fulfilled predictions of Christ were the proof of his authenticity. Peter said, "This is how God fulfilled what he had foretold through all the prophets, saying that his Christ would suffer.... Indeed, all the prophets from Samuel on, as many as have spoken, have foretold these days" (Acts 3:18, 24).

---

3   There are far too many references to deal with here. The following examples are not exhaustive: Matthew 1:22-23; 2:23; 5:17-18; 8:17; 12:17-21; 21:4-5; 26:56; Luke 18:31-33; 24:25-27; John 1:45; 12:38; 13:18-19; 15:25; Acts 13:27-29; 26:22-23; 28:23; Romans 1:2-3; 1 Peter 1:10-12; Revelation 10:7.

Similarly, Paul argued that Christ should be trusted because he fulfilled prophecies: "As his custom was, Paul went into the synagogue, and on three Sabbath days he reasoned with them from the Scriptures, explaining and proving that the Christ had to suffer and rise from the dead. 'This Jesus I am proclaiming to you is the Christ,' he said" (Acts 17:2-3).

Today, some predictions have lost their evidential value because we cannot independently verify the fulfillment. Other predictions are difficult to interpret. However, many prophecies are easy to interpret and can be independently verified, as we shall see. Other predictions are only now being fulfilled. In connection with one of these predictions, Jesus made a claim similar to that in Isaiah: "I have told you everything ahead of time" (Mark 13:23). The predictions coming true today, along with the ones fulfilled in the past, lead to a very convincing argument that God is speaking in the Bible. These fulfilled predictions cannot be explained except as a product of divine inspiration.

Strong advantages

Consider the strengths of this idea of a self-authenticating written body of predictive material foretelling subsequent history.

By using this approach, God authenticates his message without any need for a live demonstration of power to every person. We have actual manuscripts in the Dead Sea Scrolls that easily pre-date the events predicted. The authenticity of the Bible's text is further enhanced because the books were widely copied and dispersed over a period of hundreds of years. In order to do this, God chose the Jewish nation, who would take it upon themselves to write and preserve this scripture. The Israelites did an excellent job, carefully copying and guarding the biblical scrolls over a period of fifteen hundred years.

We have samples of the Old Testament Scriptures from long before the time of Christ as well as afterward. They show that the

Jews were extremely careful in the transmission of their sacred text. Scholars have shown that, with the numerous copies of the Bible we have from different areas and periods, we can rest assured that the copy we have today is very much the same as the copies dating back as far as hundreds of years before the time of Christ.[4]

Using a written record also makes sense because we won't have the experience described earlier upon seeing a miracle ("Let's see that again!"). With a written text, people can return to re-examine the evidence as often and as long as they want. Also, the teaching portions of the message are directly tied to the predictive evidence of divine inspiration because both are in the same manuscript.

If God provided a list of hundreds of predictive statements about history, we could look at the predictions and compare them with the subsequent events described. If the predictions were precisely fulfilled, we would have some real evidence to consider.

Of course, there are others who claim to be able to foretell the future, even in our own day, but they can't do it. As God stated in Isaiah:

> I am the Lord, who has made all things… who foils the signs of false prophets and makes fools of diviners, who overthrows the learning of the wise and turns it into nonsense, who carries out the words of his servants and fulfills the predictions of his messengers (Isaiah 44:24-26).

---

4   The respected archaeologist W. F. Albright said, "We may rest assured that the consonantal text of the Hebrew Bible, though not infallible, has been preserved with an accuracy perhaps unparalleled in any other Near Eastern literature." Cited in Gleason L. Archer, Jr., *A Survey of Old Testament Introduction* (Chicago: Moody Press, 1974), 67. See Albright's articles, "The Early Hebrew Manuscripts and the Early Versions" and "Lower Criticism of the Old Testament," 3-67, and R. K. Harrison, "The History of Hebrew Writing" and "The Old Testament Text," in *Introduction to the Old Testament* (Grand Rapids, Mich.: Eerdmans, 1969), 201-243. For New Testament document transmission, see F. F. Bruce, *The New Testament Documents: Are They Reliable?* (Downers Grove, Ill.: InterVarsity Press, 1960).

Phony predictions

Not all claimed predictions of the future are authentic. One source often believed to be predictive is Nostradamus. The following is an example of one of his predictions:

> The senseless ire of the furious combat will cause steel to be flashed at the table by brothers: To part them death, wound, and curiously, The proud duel will come to harm France.

This "prophecy," we are told, predicts the Camp David Accords between Israel and Egypt and the assassination of Anwar Sadat! The "table" refers to the bargaining table. The "proud duel" refers to international terrorism. The "harm to France" refers to the destabilization in the Near East since the death of Sadat.[5]

The critical reader sees no context to guide the interpretation. Believers routinely separate these stanzas from one another and analyze them independently. In fact, the saying doesn't even have syntax or grammar to indicate the meaning. Instead, the interpreter attaches to the words any meaning he desires. The idea that a reference to brothers at a table in 1555 refers to these two men in 1978 is really absurd. It's ludicrous because we are given no reason to follow the far-out interpretation other than vague word association.

In the next few pages, notice how different biblical predictions are. Remember, God gave us this evidence because he loves us. He wants us to know he is there and that he is involved in the flow of history. He is not catering to our curiosity. He is calling us to realize the implications of what we see and to turn to him.

---

5   Jean-Charles de Fontbrune, *Nostradamus: Countdown to Apocalypse* (New York: Holt, Rinehart and Winston, 1980), p. 52. This text is from Century II Q 34. Fortbrune does not translate Nostradamus accurately into English. See the correct translation of the text in Edgar Leoni, *Nostradamus and His Prophecies* (New York: Bell Publishing Company, 1961), p. 171.

CHAPTER 4

The Time of Jesus' Coming Predicted

Scores of historical predictions in the Old Testament have come true. Those of particular interest to us are the predictions that:

1. Foretell events or persons with extreme accuracy

2. Predict unique or very unusual events that make coincidence implausible

3. Can be independently verified, and

4. Would have been impossible to fake or counterfeit.

In the ancient book of Daniel we have a passage that is astonishing in its detail and accuracy: the prophecy of the "seventy sevens" in chapter 9. People don't teach it as often for one simple reason: it is complicated. Yet precisely this fact makes it remarkable. This is what the passage says:

A period of seventy sets of seven has been decreed for your people and your holy city to finish their rebellion, to put an end to their sin, to atone for their guilt, to bring in everlasting righteousness, to confirm the prophetic vision, and to anoint the Most Holy Place. Now listen and understand! Seven sets of seven plus sixty-two sets of seven will pass from the time the command is given to rebuild Jerusalem until a ruler—the Anointed One—comes. Jerusalem will be rebuilt with streets and strong defenses, despite the perilous times. After this period of sixty-two sets of seven, the Anointed One will be killed, appearing to have accomplished nothing, and a ruler will arise whose armies will destroy the city and the Temple. The end will come with a flood, and war and its miseries are decreed from that time to the very end (Daniel 9:24-26).

In 539 B.C., we are told, a messenger from God came to Daniel with the vision above. The term "sevens" throughout the passage refers to Hebrew "sabbatical years," or seven year units of time. This is clear from the earlier part of the chapter.[6] In verse 24 it says that 490 years have been allowed by God for the Jewish people to, among other things, "bring in everlasting righteousness." Then the years are broken down into sections. In verse 25 he explained that: "From the issuing of the decree... until the Anointed One, the ruler... will be seven 'sevens' [49 years], and sixty-two 'sevens' [434 years]."

This "Anointed One" (Hebrew for "Messiah") who will "put an end to sin," "atone for wickedness," and "bring in everlasting righ-

---

6 Earlier in this same chapter, Daniel says he read in the book of Jeremiah that God sent the nation of Israel into exile for seventy years because they had disobeyed the Law of Moses. He discovered that God set the length of the exile at seventy years because of the law of the seventh (Sabbath) year in Leviticus (also stated in 2 Chronicles 36:21). God had warned that if Israel disobeyed his covenant, he would scatter them "among the nations.... Then the land will enjoy its sabbath years all the time that it lies desolate and you are in the country of your enemies; then the land will rest and enjoy its sabbaths" (Leviticus 26:33-34). Daniel 9:11 also refers to this passage. Forsaking the sabbatical year was not the only sin Israel was guilty of during this period. They also committed sexual immorality, idolatry, and human sacrifice, to name a few. The sabbatical year seems to have been used to set the *length* of the exile, not the *fact* of the exile.

teousness" is none other than the world Savior so often promised in the Old Testament.

This passage is amazing because it not only says such a savior will come, it also says exactly *when* he will come!

Remember, the book of Daniel was written more than five hundred years before the time of Christ. As a matter of fact, we have eight different manuscripts from Daniel in the Dead Sea Scrolls and other sources that predate Christ.[7]

So when should he come?

What date, then, does Daniel name for the coming of the world Savior? Amazingly, the prophecy begins in the fifth century B.C. and ends during the ministry of Jesus of Nazareth in the first half of the first century A.D.! The exact dates for the fulfillment can be worked out a couple of ways, but the outcome is never in doubt. Jesus Christ was predicted in a unique way centuries before he was born.

Dating Daniel's prophecy

To assign a date for the fulfillment of the seventy weeks prediction, we must determine the length of time predicted, the beginning point, and then the end.

---

7 Skeptics have challenged some of the predictions in Daniel in recent years, claiming that Daniel may have been written after some of the events predicted. If that were true, the book would really be only history, not prophecy. However, no one can claim Daniel 9 originated after the time of Christ. See a radical late-dating of Daniel to 160 B.C. in S. B. Frost, "Daniel," *The Interpreter's Dictionary of the Bible,* 1 (New York: Abingdon Press, 1962), 761-768. This skeptical scholar admits, however, "That Daniel was widely recognized as scripture from the second and first centuries B.C. onward can be in no doubt." (762). Qumran (Q4) contained a commentary on Daniel and Daniel appears in the Septuagint, the Greek translation of the Old Testament from around 180 BC. Also 1 Maccabees (which is no later in origin than 135 B.C.) refers to Daniel (2:59-60). S. B. Frost, *Daniel,The Interpreter's Dictionary of the Bible,* 1, 763.) It should be clear, therefore, that Daniel could not have known what would happen in the first century A.D., regardless of whose dating we accept.

- The length of the interval:

Observe again the wording of the prophecy:

> From the issuing of the decree ... until the Anointed One, the ruler ... will be seven 'sevens' [49 years], and sixty-two 'sevens' [434 years]" (9:25).

We see the "from... until" language here that specifies an interval of 49 plus 434 years, or a total of 483 years.

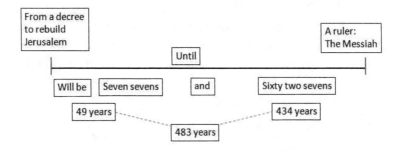

- The beginning point:

The beginning point is a "decree to rebuild Jerusalem," which was in ruins at the time Daniel wrote. The issuing of this decree is recorded in Nehemiah 2:1-10, along with its exact date, during the reign of Artaxerxes I.[8]

---

8 Notice that the decree mentioned in Daniel 9 is to rebuild the city of Jerusalem, not the temple. It also mentions building the city's defenses. Daniel 9:25: "It will be built again, with plaza and moat" (NASB). These facts distinguish this decree from several others issued in connection with rebuilding the temple only. However, even if we were to date the beginning of the vision to an earlier decree mentioned in Ezra 4:11-12, 23, the outcome would lead directly to the life and ministry of Jesus Christ. This is how scholars like J. Barton Payne understand the prediction. When handled this way, the ending date turns out to be A.D. 26. This, he argues, would have been the first year of Jesus' ministry. J. Barton Payne, *Encyclopedia of Biblical Prophecy* (New York: Harper & Row, 1973) 382-388. This approach to the vision is certainly plausible. However, I believe that the approach outlined here is more accurate for the reasons given below.

Any encyclopedia will show that Artaxerxes I was king of Persia from 465 – 424 B.C. Since the month of Nisan is in the spring, the actual date of this decree issued in the twentieth year of the king's reign was March/April 444 B.C.[9]

Not even skeptical historians question this date for the Jews' return from captivity in Babylon to Jerusalem. The return is well-attested by independent sources. Remember, Nehemiah was also written hundreds of years before the time of Jesus, so it was not possible for him to "fix" the date.

- The target date:

The Hebrew year is 360 days (12 months of 30 days each), which is a total of 173,880 days. This is approximately 476 of our years. Since there is no such thing as a "0" year in our calendar, we need to deduct one more year from the difference.[10] Subtracting, we get 444 - 476 = -32 - 1 = -33. The negative number indicates an A.D. date. In other words, when Hebrew lunar years are converted to modern solar years, this passage

---

9 The Persian king's years were dated according to the "accession-year" system. In this system, ancients did not count the first partial calendar year of a king's reign, although we do count it. Because 465 would have been a partial year, Nisan (the first month of the year in their calendar) in the twentieth year of this king would have been in 444 B.C. The sometimes complicated procedures for reconciling ancient calendars are explained in detail in Jack Finnegan, *Handbook of Biblical Chronology: Principles of Time Reckoning in the Ancient World and Problems of Chronology in the Bible* (Princeton, N.J.: Princeton University Press, 1964), 82-86.

10 By looking at this diagram, you can see the difference between a calendar (on top) and a number line (below):

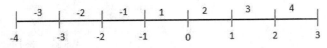

Notice how the points line up before 0, but are one apart after 0. That's because calendars count years (the spaces between points) while normal math counts the points. This is why we need to compensate one year for the non-existing 0 year.

predicts that the Messiah would come in A.D. 33! The more accurately the conversion is worked out, the more accurate the result.[11]

The best year for the fulfillment of Daniel's prophecy is A.D. 33. In the month of Nisan in A.D. 33, Jesus entered Jerusalem on a donkey's colt. This was the entry predicted by Zechariah:

> Rejoice greatly, O daughter of Zion! Shout, daughter of Jerusalem! See, your king comes to you, righteous and having salvation, gentle and riding on a donkey, on a colt, the foal of a donkey." (Zechariah 9:9)

What about trickery?

These two predictions form an interesting comparison. Someone could fake the one in Zechariah if he wanted to pretend he was the Messiah. He could just ride a donkey colt into Jerusalem while having his friends acclaim him as king. But Jesus *could not* have faked the prediction in Daniel, even if he had a motive for being the suffering Messiah.[12]

With the advent of modern archaeology we are now able to determine the exact dates for events in the latter part of the Old Testament (like the decree to rebuild Jerusalem) with far more accuracy than anyone could at the time of Christ. It would have been impossible for people at the time of Christ to determine the exact year this prophecy was fulfilled because accurate records had not been kept. The

---

11 Scholars such as Harold W. Hoehner have argued that this prediction points to the exact day of the Triumphal Entry of Christ. His conclusion rests on the assumption that when the day of the month is not given (as in Nehemiah) the first day should be assumed. Then the remainder is worked out to six digits and compared to solunar tables that give us the month indicated in A.D. 33. Harold W. Hoehner, "Chronological Aspects of the Life of Christ," Part 4: 'Daniel's Seventy Weeks and New Testament Chronology,' *Biblioteca Sacra*, 132, 525 (Jan.-Mar. 1975), pp. 46-65.

12 Daniel 9:26 says "the Anointed One will be killed" (or "cut off," NASB, an idiom short for "cut off out of the land of the living," i.e. killed) so this isn't a prophecy that someone would want to fulfill.

people in Jesus' day were aware that the prophecy of Daniel was due to be fulfilled soon, as witnessed by the ancient historian Josephus.[13] However, they were only aware that Messiah should come within a generation or so.

One other objection could be raised to this prediction: could the Gospel authors have lied about the entire event? For several good reasons, the answer is no.

In the first place, the Gospel records never actually give the date of Christ's death. Scholars base this date on other data in the Gospels that can be cross-checked with external sources. For instance, Pilate had to be in Galilee at the time of Jesus' death. Also, Herod's temple had been under construction for 46 years at the beginning of Jesus' ministry (John 2:20). These data and others enable historians to determine that only April A.D. 30 or April A.D. 33 would meet all of the New Testament requirements. The latter date better accounts for the events mentioned in the Gospels.[14] Therefore, by correctly describing the situation in A.D. 33, the Gospel authors indirectly identified the correct circumstances surrounding the fulfillment of this prediction.

This means that for the authors of the Gospels to fake this passage, they not only would have to know the date they were faking, but they also would have to know what criteria modern scholars would use to fix a date for the event! Besides, if they wanted to fake a date, wouldn't they simply name that date in the usual way?[15] But this never happened.

---

13 Josephus says, "This oracle [Daniel 9] certainly denoted the government of Vespasian, who was appointed emperor in Judea." Flavius Josephus, *The Jewish War*, 4, 5, 4. But Vespasian would have been almost forty years off the correct date. This shows how close they could come at that time.

14 Only the A.D. 33 date can explain the timid behavior of Pilate when threatened by the mob (John 19:12-16). Since he had been appointed by the Roman traitor Sejanus, who was found out in November A.D. 31, Pilate was in danger of being executed as a traitor. The purge of officials appointed by Sejanus was in full swing in A.D. 33. See Gary DeLashmutt, "Sejanus,"*The Xenos Journal*, Vol. 2, #2, 49-61. See also Harold Hoehner, "Chronological Aspects," *Biblioteca Sacra*, 132, 155 (Jan.-Mar. 1975) 46-65.

15 Dates were based on the events happening in the Roman Empire at this time, particularly the acclamations voted to the emperor. Thus, a year might be described as "the year of the thirty-second imperator acclamation."

The Gospel authors had no accurate calendar information on which to base a faked record, so how could they have been this accurate? In other words, we can't account for the accuracy of the prediction by claiming that the Gospel authors lied, because they would not have been able to lie this accurately! Neither would they have known the techniques we, in the modern world, use to assign accurate dates to events in their day. So if the New Testament authors had desired to lie about the fulfillment of Daniel 9, they would have found it impossible to do so.

Finally, even without any Gospel records, we would be able to determine that the essential facts in Daniel's prediction came true. We know from the ancient Roman historian Tacitus and the ancient Jewish historian Josephus that Jesus, founder of the Christian sect, was crucified by Pontius Pilate in Judea.[16] These secular sources had nothing to gain by referring to Jesus. They refer to him because their sources indicated that his life was a historical fact.

Even without the statements these witnesses made about Jesus, we would know Jesus must have lived at about this time. This is because the Christian movement appeared with some force by the middle of the first century. Allowing a number of years for development indicates the founder (Jesus) must have lived sometime shortly before or after A.D. 30. We can narrow the date further by noting that Pilate would have been in Judea to execute Jesus only during that same period of time. This is why historians today do not doubt the existence of Jesus at about A.D. 30.

The big picture

As we add up the evidence, then, we see that:

1. There was such a person as Jesus of Nazareth who was cruci-
    fied by Pontius Pilate.

---

16 Josephus, *Jewish Antiquities,* 18, 3, 3. See also Tacitus, who includes the observation that Jesus was crucified by Pontius Pilate, *Annals,* 15, 44.

2. Historians give the best date for his death at A.D. 33.

3. Even without reference to any Christian accounts, we can date the event to the same general time.

4. It would have been impossible to come up with such an accurate date for the fulfillment of Daniel's prophecy based on the knowledge available at the time of Christ's death.

What are the chances that the Old Testament prophet Daniel would predict, to the year, the coming of the man the History Channel calls "the most influential person in human history"? Even if we accepted the secular dating for Daniel (160 B.C.) instead of Daniel's own dating (539 B.C.), he would have no way to know this. Is it really reasonable to think that his prediction of Jesus' coming was a lucky guess? But if not a guess, what is the explanation?

The more you think about Daniel 9, the more you realize you can't give any convincing naturalistic explanation for this remarkable prophecy. The prediction:

a. was written hundreds of years before it was fulfilled,

b. is detailed and amazingly exact,

c. could not have been faked by a false Messiah or his followers, and

d. its fulfillment can be independently verified.

It is, in other words, exactly what God said he would provide: evidence that he is uniquely speaking in the Bible. No other book, ancient or modern, has anything like this. Don't believe false claims that other books have predictive prophecy that came true like the Bible. I've been researching such claims for years and have yet to find anything even remotely similar to the authentic prophecy in the Bible. God said in Isaiah 6, "I am God, and there is none like me. I make known the end from the beginning, from ancient times, what is still to come" (vs. 9). Truly, only God could do this.

Don't miss the focal point for this prediction, either: Jesus Christ was pre-authenticated in a way no other founder of any faith was. Because his life, deeds, family, date, death, and resurrection were all predicted in advance, and in detail, he gains a supernatural credibility that nobody else can claim. What an ingenious way to demonstrate divine inspiration!

As you read about the fulfillment of Daniel's prediction, you may be sensing that this is mind-blowing confirmation spoken by God. As you read on, you will find a growing body of evidence, like layers that become increasingly persuasive. Eventually, you may have a desire to know more by taking a step of faith as described earlier—to open the cupboard door and see if the peanut butter is there. It's never too soon to take your search to God in person. God's love and his desire to enter into a personal relationship with you is what prompted him to reveal this demonstration of his existence and desire to communicate.

CHAPTER 5

Isaiah's
Remarkable Predictions

We have already seen some passages in Isaiah where God claims to tell the future as a way to demonstrate authentic self-revelation. In the very section of Isaiah where he makes these claims, a series of fascinating predictions serve as examples. The most interesting of these prophecies are known as the Anonymous Servant Songs—four Hebrew poems that paint a picture of one known only as "the servant of the Lord."[17]

---

17 The four passages are Isaiah 42:1-9; 49:1-13; 50:4-11; and 52:13-53:12. Although God makes other predictions involving his "servant Israel" in this part of Isaiah, these four passages are clearly about a human servant rather than the nation of Israel for the following reasons:

> a. Isaiah 49:1: The servant is called "from the womb" (NASB).

> b. Isaiah 53:2-6: The contrast is made between "he" and "him" versus "we." The author (Isaiah) is Jewish, so the "we" must refer to the Jewish nation, or to the human race, including the Jewish nation. The servant is also contrasted to "my people" (the Jews) in 53:8.

We give a detailed accounting of the passages later, but here is a summary of Isaiah's portrait of this servant:

> A savior will one day come who will be filled with the Spirit of God. He will begin his ministry in obscurity rather than with the majesty people expect of such a savior. Indeed, this savior will be rejected by his own people. He will suffer persecution and torture. Although he teaches the Word of God, his contemporaries will believe that God is against him. Finally, the servant will be killed, but in dying, he will pay the price that the human race should have to pay for sin. After a period of time he will rise from the dead, and bring multitudes into close relationship with God based on his work. Eventually, he will be crowned as a king, and even the other kings of the earth will be subject to him.

These prophecies were written hundreds of years before the time of Jesus. In fact, the oldest biblical scroll discovered so far is the 250 B.C. manuscript of Isaiah from the Dead Sea Scrolls. Because they so precisely describe Jesus' work, they, like Daniel, pre-authenticate Jesus. Most of the events described were not under Jesus' control, so they couldn't have been faked. Also, the rabbis didn't even understand these passages to be referring to the expected Messiah at the time Christ lived, because they didn't realize there were two comings for the Messiah.[18] So it would have been both impossible and point-

---

c. The servant is said to be "the redeemer of Israel" (49:7), and he will "bring Jacob back to [God], in order that Israel might be gathered to Him... and to restore the preserved ones of Israel" (49:5-6).

d. The servant is called a "man" in 53:3 (see also 52:14; 53:8, 11).

e. Isaiah 53:8: The servant dies. But death is never predicted for the Jewish people. Rather, they will never pass away (cf. Is. 55:9-10).

f. The servant is completely obedient and righteous, unlike the people of Israel, who are often chided for their sin—even in the servant songs themselves (see Isaiah 50:5: "I was not disobedient," and Isaiah 53:9: "He had done no violence, nor was there any deceit in His mouth").

18   This is probably one reason why the servant is never identified by name in Isaiah.

less for Christ to deliberately fulfill these predictions. It would have been impossible because he had no way to obtain cooperation from the Roman and Jewish authorities who fulfilled the predictions by their actions. It would have been pointless because the predictions include the requirement that he be tortured to death. Why would someone want to fulfill that?

The New Testament makes it clear that these passages refer to Jesus (see Matthew 8:17; 12:17-21; Acts 8:32-33). Would it be possible that his followers lied to make it seem like he fulfilled these predictions? That's implausible. Modern scholars agree that the life and the death of Jesus were real historical events. There is too much evidence to ignore, including sources outside the Bible, as we saw in the previous chapter. And again, why would early Christians fabricate a dying leader when that picture flew directly in the face of everything their culture expected from the Messiah? Instead, we have a sort of coded set of predictions that are clear today, but which left enough ambiguity so that Jesus' enemies persecuted and killed him without realizing they were acting according to the plan.

We find in these passages a remarkable description of the life and ministry of Jesus Christ written centuries before his birth. It's particularly striking to read Isaiah 53 from beginning to end. That chapter is describing clearly, to even a first-time reader, the life of Jesus Christ.

It seems that God wanted to present the material in such a way that those opposing Jesus would not realize they were actually assisting God's plan when they put him to death. Only after the life and death of Christ did the full meaning of these prophecies become clear. Yet Christians are not misinterpreting the passages after the fact, because the passages cannot be made to fit any other person or group. The rabbis had debated the meaning of these passages for centuries before the coming of Christ, but they could not reconcile this picture of the suffering and dying servant with the picture of the triumphant "King Messiah" spoken of in passages such as Isaiah 9:6ff. The result was that some rabbis proposed two possible Messiahs. We now know that there are not two Messiahs, but two comings of the same Messiah. See a full explanation in Dennis McCallum, *Satan and His Kingdom: What the Bible Says and How it Matters to You*, (Minneapolis MN: Bethany House Publishing, 2007) Ch. 4, 5. See what the rabbis thought about these passages at the time of Christ in H. H. Rowley, *The Servant of the Lord and Other Essays on the Old Testament* (London: Latterworth Press, 1952), pp. 61-87.

The 'Anonymous Servant' in Isaiah

Here is a more detailed breakdown of the servant of the Lord as portrayed in the Servant Songs.

1. He is filled with the Holy Spirit: "I will put my Spirit upon Him" (Isaiah 42:1; cf. Luke 4:1).

2. He begins his ministry in obscurity and apparent failure.

   a. "In the shadow of His hand He has concealed Me... He has hidden Me in His quiver" (Isaiah 49:2).

   b. "I have toiled in vain" (Isaiah 49:4).

   c. "He has no stately form or majesty that we should look upon Him, nor appearance that we should be attracted to Him" (Isaiah 53:2).

3. The servant executes a prophetic or teaching ministry.

   a. "He will faithfully bring forth justice" (Isaiah 42:3). This indicates definitive decision or judgment.

   b. They "will wait... for His [oral] law" (Isaiah 42:4). Torah, here translated "law," also means "teaching."

   c. "I will appoint you... a light to the nations" (Isaiah 42:6). He will be used to bring God's knowledge to Gentiles.

   d. His obedience results in the ability to teach "faithfully and effectively" (Isaiah 50:4).

4. The servant is humiliated and persecuted.

   a. The servant is voluntarily smitten, has his beard plucked, is spat upon, and is humiliated" (Isaiah 50:6).

   b. His appearance is "terribly marred" (Isaiah 52:14).

   c. He is despised, forsaken, sorrowful, and grief-stricken (Isaiah 53:3).

d. The servant is afflicted, bearing grief and sorrows (Isaiah 53:4).

e. He is oppressed and afflicted (Isaiah 53:7).

f. He is put to grief (Isaiah 53:10).

g. He is crushed and scourged (Isaiah 53:5).

5. The servant is killed and buried (Isaiah 53:8-9).

Note the seemingly incomprehensible statement "His grave was assigned with wicked men, yet He was with a rich man in His death" (53:9). This is an accurate description of the burial of Jesus. As a victim of crucifixion, he should have been thrown into a common pit for criminals. But instead, Joseph of Arimathea obtained Jesus' body from Pilate and placed it in a hand-hewn tomb—something only the rich could afford (John 19:38-41).

6. He atones for the sins of others by a substitutionary death (i.e., he dies in their place).

a. "Thus He will sprinkle many nations" (Isaiah 52:15). This is a reference to ritual sprinkling of blood as practiced in the Old Testament (cf. Exodus 29:16).

b. The servant "bears our griefs and sorrows" (Isaiah 53:4).

c. The servant is "pierced through for our transgressions, He was crushed for our iniquities; the chastening for our well-being fell upon Him" (Isaiah 53:5).

d. "The Lord has caused the iniquity of us all to fall on Him" (Isaiah 53:6).

e. "He was cut off from the land of the living, for the transgression of my people, to whom the stroke was due" (Isaiah 53:8).

f. God renders the servant as a "guilt offering" for others' sins. This refers to Old Testament sacrificial ritual (Isaiah 53:10; cf. Leviticus 5:15).

g. "My Servant will justify the many, as He will bear their iniquities" (Isaiah 53:11).

h. "He poured out Himself to death, and was numbered with the transgressors; yet He Himself bore the sin of many, and interceded for the transgressors" (Isaiah 53:12).

7. He is raised from the dead:

"He [God] will prolong his days" (Isaiah 53:10)—this, after the servant is dead and buried (vs. 8, 9).

8. The servant's death leads to an ongoing ministry with his followers or "offspring from all nations."

a. The servant sets captives free (Isaiah 42:7; 49:9; 42:25).

b. He establishes a new covenant (Isaiah 42:6; 49:8).

c. He will see his offspring (Isaiah 53:10).

c. He will reconcile both Jews and Gentiles to God (Isaiah 49:5-6).

9. He is glorified.

a. "Kings shall see and arise" (Isaiah 49:7)—standing up was a way of paying tribute. Kings never stood for a visitor; the visitor never sat down in the presence of a king.

b. "Kings will shut their mouths on account of Him" (Isaiah 52:15).

c. "I will allot Him a portion with the great" (Isaiah 53:12).

Other aspects of Jesus' life predicted

Many other prophecies in the Old Testament verify the claims of Christ; in fact, far too many to detail here. Briefly, here is a partial list of some of the typical predictions and their fulfillments. Note that many of these features were not under Jesus' control, so he could not have fulfilled them on purpose.

- Birthplace (Micah 5:2).

  Micah named Jesus' birthplace in advance. Only the small village of Bethlehem could be the birthplace of the Messiah. Events from the second coming of Christ are also mentioned in this passage, including the eventual takeover of the world.[19]

- Betrayal (Zechariah 11:12-14).

  Judas' betrayal of Jesus is predicted in one passage where God is portrayed as a "foolish shepherd." For the purpose of communication, the prophet, Zechariah, acted out the betrayal and, remarkably, mentions the actual figure of "thirty pieces of silver." God says with sad irony that this "magnificent sum" (the price of a slave) was the value the people placed on him.

  The New Testament teaches that this divine drama predicts Judas' betrayal of Jesus (Matthew 26:15). Notice that Zechariah also predicts that the money would finally be thrown into the temple and given to a potter. This actually happened when, after Judas threw the thirty pieces into the temple, the priests used that money to buy land from a local potter as a cemetery.

- Crucifixion (Psalm 22:6-18).

---

19   This conflating of the two comings of Jesus probably led to the impression that he was only coming once (although that is never stated). This worked against enemies, especially Satan, who mistakenly cooperated in his death (1 Cor. 2:8).

Jesus' death by crucifixion was described in detail centuries before crucifixion had been invented! The details include the fact that:

- ✓ His hands and feet were pierced (v. 16).
- ✓ He was naked (v. 17).
- ✓ His bones were being pulled out of joint (v. 14).
- ✓ His thirst was so intense that his tongue stuck to his jaws (v. 15).
- ✓ He was encircled by taunting persecutors as he died (v. 12, 13, 17).
- ✓ Men gambled for his clothing while he watched (v. 18).

Notice Jesus quoted the first verse of this psalm while on the cross: "My God, my God, why have you forsaken me?" He was calling the people's attention to his fulfillment of this well-known psalm before their eyes. At the same time, he literally was being forsaken by God at that moment as the judgment for human sin fell upon him.

- Lineage (Matthew 1:1-16; Luke 3:23-38).

Jesus' lineage was spelled out in detail hundreds of years before his birth. We also discover a fascinating apparent contradiction here which must have seemed irreconcilable. Yet all the requirements were fulfilled. According to the Old Testament, the Messiah must be:

- ✓ A descendant of Abraham (Genesis 12:3)
- ✓ A descendant of Isaac, not Ishmael (Genesis 21:12)
- ✓ A member of the tribe of Judah rather than any of the other eleven tribes (Genesis 49:10)
- ✓ A descendant of David rather than any of the hundreds of other families in the tribe of Judah (Isaiah 9:6)
- ✓ A descendant of the kingly line of Solomon rather than any of the hundreds of other children in this huge family (2 Samuel 7:13)

✓ Yet, he could not be a descendant of Jeconiah, one of the
   kings in this very line (Jeremiah 22:28)

A careful reading of the two records of Jesus' lineage reveals
that they are not the same. Both agree up until the time of
King David. But Matthew says it was Solomon who gave rise
to the line of Christ, while Luke says it was another son of
David, Nathan, who gave rise to the line of the Messiah.

The resolution of this quandary is found in verse 23 of Luke's
account. There it says Jesus was "supposedly the son of Joseph,
the son of Eli." In fact, this phrase should be taken to mean
that Jesus was "supposedly the son of Joseph (who, according
to the claim of a virgin birth, was not Jesus' birth father) but
was really the son of Mary."

Eli was Mary's father, not Joseph's father. (Women were routinely left out of these lists in the ancient world.) Therefore,
Matthew and Luke are different because they trace Jesus'
lineage through different parents. Matthew recounts Joseph's
lineage, and Luke recounts Mary's.

As a result, Jesus fit all the requirements for the Messiah's
lineage, even though those requirements seemed contradictory.

- ✓ He was in the line of David and was a blood descendant
  of David's through Mary, which fulfills the Davidic
  covenant.
- ✓ He was not a blood descendant of Jeconiah who was
  accursed and his descendants disallowed from sitting on
  the throne of David according to Jeremiah.
- ✓ He was entitled to be a part of the kingly line of David,
  including the right to be a king in that line, through
  inheritance from his adoptive father, Joseph.

So, even though the requirements for Messiah in Old Testament prophecy seemed self-contradictory, Jesus fulfilled all of
them. This is no coincidence!

The big picture

Can any other founder of a known religion point to a similar written record of his life already in existence hundreds of years before his birth? Would it have been possible, for instance, for Mohammad (the founder of Islam), Sakyamuni (Buddha), or Lao-tzu (the founder of Taoism) to point to a place in an already existing, widely known and read book and see there a listing of the unique features of his life?

No.

No other founder of a world religion could point to such pre-authentication of his ministry. Jesus alone is able to say, "Everything must be fulfilled that is written about me in the Law of Moses, the Prophets and the Psalms" (Luke 24:44). The uniqueness of Jesus is as real as the uniqueness of God himself, who said: "I am God, and there is no other.... I make known the end from the beginning, from ancient times, what is still to come" (Isaiah 46:9-10).

CHAPTER 6

This Has Never
Happened Before

The Old and New Testament prophets agreed that history will move toward a climax. This climax will occur just before the personal return of Christ. Then, history as we know it will come to an end and God will take over the world from that time on. This pattern could be called a "linear" view of history, because it has a beginning and an end.

Such a view of history is very different from that held by most religions. Religions usually teach that history is going through repetitive cycles. They believe human history will be either eternal or extremely long—some claim millions of years into the future.[20]

Most scholars are convinced that these circular views of history

---

20   Mircea Eliade, *Myths, Dreams and Mysteries* (London: Harvill Press, 1957), p. 49. See also his discussion of the universal "belief in a time that is cyclic, in an eternal returning, in the periodic destruction of the world and mankind to be followed by a new world and a new, regenerated mankind." (Mircea Eliade, *Patterns in Comparative Religion* (New York: New American Library, 1974), 407.

derive from the seasonal cycles in nature and birth-fertility-death cycles. Religious thinkers project the course of nature onto history. In agrarian or hunter-gatherer societies, where nothing changes for hundreds of years, such cyclical theories were plausible.[21]

However, as human history has developed, we now realize that cyclical views of history are simply wrong. Human history is clearly moving in directions that have never happened before. For instance, the world has never experienced a period of highly developed technology or population density in supposed previous cycles of history. Instead of cycles, we now see history conforming to the pattern predicted in the Bible. History is clearly moving toward a climax different from anything in earlier times.

Not only is the Bible correct about the linear pattern of history, it also goes into great detail about events at the end of history as we know it. Some of these events are happening in our own day. These amazing predictions have the same effect as those we saw earlier—they show that the Bible is all alone as a validated source of supernatural insight from God.

A completely unique prediction

The ancient prophet Isaiah wrote:

> In that day the Lord will reach out his hand a second time to reclaim the remnant that is left of his people from Assyria, from Lower Egypt, from Upper Egypt, from Cush, from Elam, from Babylonia, from Hamath and from the islands of the sea (Isaiah 11:11).[22]

---

21 This is why, in most religions, the new year festival is the premier festival of the year. (Harold Turner, "Holy Places, Sacred Calendars," in R. Pierce Beaver et. al., eds., *Eerdmans' Handbook to the World's Religions,* (Grand Rapids, MI.: Eerdmans, 1982), 20-21. Interestingly, biblical teaching apparently doesn't even have a New Year festival. Passover is in Nisan, which is the first month of the year (Exodus 12:2). However, it is on the fourteenth day of the month (Exodus 12:6). The New Year held no great significance for the ancient Hebrews.

22 The "islands of the sea" refers to distant lands that lay beyond the ocean. It is sometimes translated "coastlands."

Correlation

This world-wide regathering of the nation of Israel after their nation ceased to exist for thousands of years is one of the most frequently predicted events in the Bible. This is an important point, because if something was only predicted once, people might misinterpret the passage. But in biblical prophecy, key predictions are repeated multiple times in different books, making the intention very clear. This is called correlation—parallel statements in unrelated literary settings. It's an important feature of authentic prophecy that is completely lacking in pseudo-prophecies like what we saw earlier in Nostradamus.[23]

These parallel passages are well worth studying in their own context, although we won't have space to do so here: Deuteronomy 4:27-30; 28:64-5; 30:1-6; Isaiah 11:11–16; 27:12-13; 43:5-7; 66:19-20; Jeremiah 3:14-18; 16:14-15; 23:3-8; 30:3, 10-11; 32:37-44; Ezekiel 11:16-20; 20:41-42; 28:25; 34:12-14; 37:11-12, 14, 21-22, 25; 38:8; 39:25-29; Hosea 1:11; 3:4-5; 11:10-11; Micah 2:12-13; 4:6; 5:2-4; 7:9-13; Zephaniah 3:18-20; Zechariah 8:3, 7, 20-22; 10:9-12.

The earliest promise

In one of the earliest books, Moses warned that the day was coming when, "the Lord will scatter you among all peoples, from one end of the earth to the other end of the earth..." (Deuteronomy 28:64). But then he goes on to predict an amazing regathering into their own land:

> Then the Lord your God will restore you from captivity, and
> have compassion on you, and will gather you again from all

---

23   The plentitude of passages on Israel's regathering are complicated by the strange fact that Israel has been regathered to their land no fewer than three times! The first was in Exodus, when they were delivered from Egypt. The second was when they returned after being exiled in Babylon in the 500's BC. The predictions of regathering from Babylon could be confused with the predictions of the great worldwide regathering of the last days. In general, any regathering that comes from all directions and all nations must refer to the one in the twentieth century. These couldn't refer to the regathering from Babylon, which was a few thousand people, all coming from one country and one direction to Israel.

the peoples where the Lord your God has scattered you. If your outcasts are at the ends of the earth, from there the Lord your God will gather you, and from there He will bring you back. The Lord your God will bring you into the land which your fathers possessed, and you shall possess it; and He will prosper you and multiply you more than your fathers (30:3-5).

All the way back in the time of Moses, before the Jewish people even had possession of their land, this startling prediction was made. It refers to events more than *three thousand years* after the writing of the text!

Ezekiel

Again, God showed Ezekiel a vision of a vast valley filled with dried bones of dead people. Then, they began to assemble into skeletons, flesh grew on the bones, and finally, skin. Now the valley was full of corpses. Only a second prophecy summoning the breath of God caused the dead people to come to life and stand "on their feet, an exceedingly great army" (Ezekiel 37:10). God went on to explain:

> Son of man, these bones are the whole house of Israel; behold, they say, "Our bones are dried up and our hope has perished…" Thus says the Lord God, "Behold, I will open your graves and cause you to come up out of your graves, My people; and I will bring you into the land of Israel" (vs. 11, 12).[24]

This concept—that a nation could be scattered all over the earth for hundreds, even thousands of years, persecuted bitterly, and then be regathered to their ancestral homeland—is utterly unprecedented in human history. Nothing like that *has ever happened to any nation or people.* Many ancient nations were scattered and disappeared; most

---

24 This is an example of a passage clearly not referring to the Jews' return to Israel from Babylon, because in this case the Jews were scattered to nations in every direction from Israel: "I will take the sons of Israel from among the nations where they have gone, and I will gather them from every side and bring them into their own land" (37:21).

of those appearing in the Old Testament, like the Philistines, the Moabites, and the Ammonites, are all gone. The Jews should have been like them, but God said no. He would gather them from every country and bring them back to their ancient homeland.

Jesus

In 33 A.D. Jesus warned that Jerusalem would soon be destroyed (Luke 21:20) and that its inhabitants "will fall by the edge of the sword, and will be led captive into all the nations; and Jerusalem will be trampled under foot by the Gentiles until the times of the Gentiles are fulfilled" (Luke 21:24). Notice the last phrase and the word "until." This gentile ownership of Jerusalem was only temporary. After the "times of the Gentiles," Jerusalem would again become a Jewish city.[25]

In A.D. 70, the Roman general, Titus Vespasian, besieged Jerusalem and eventually burned the city. The Romans completely leveled the temple just as Jesus had predicted (Matthew 24:2). They killed many of the Jews in Jerusalem and sold the rest as slaves. Jerusalem fell under the power of Gentiles, as Jesus said it would. This situation lasted until 1967, when the Jews finally recaptured Jerusalem.

The regathering of Israel was a precondition for the other events predicted in Luke 21. It was also pivotal in the program of God because, according to verse 24, it signaled that "the times of the Gentiles are fulfilled." The events going on in Israel today are directly fulfilling prophecies uttered more than twenty centuries ago.

---

25 Note that Bible prophecy predicts both good and evil events. The fact that it predicts the retaking of Jerusalem by the Israelis is not in itself a moral commentary on all actions taken by the Israelis. In fact, some unjustifiable actions may well have occurred there. Jesus only says it will happen, not that it is morally correct. This is evident from the fact that the destruction of Jewish society by the Romans is also predicted in the same passage.

The big picture

So, in our own day we see the fulfillment of a batch of predictions that:

      ✓   are now thousands of years old

      ✓   foretell something that has never happened to any other people in history

      ✓   have been fulfilled literally and undeniably, and

      ✓   could not be faked or deliberately fulfilled.

In a word, the best explanation for this prediction is that it comes from a supernatural, all-knowing source.

When confronted with this series of predictions about the regathering of Israel, the only answer skeptics suggest is that the Jews must have purposefully fulfilled the prophecies they knew were in the Old Testament. But before jumping on this foolish explanation, consider some of the massive problems it faces:

1. If it's that easy for a people to reacquire their ancient homeland, why hasn't anyone else done it? Wouldn't the Cherokee or the Mohicans like to have their lands back? Of course they would. The Kurds in Turkey and Iraq have been trying to get a homeland for centuries without success.

2. If the Jews self-fulfilled these prophecies simply because they believed them, why did they wait two thousand years to do so?

3. How did the Jews manage to get the United Nations to vote their country into existence, including nations like the USSR, which could have vetoed the resolution single-handed? Why would such an atheistic government join a conspiracy to fulfill prophecy from the Bible?

4. Why were most of the founders of Zionism non-believers in God or the Bible? The movement began under the leadership of socialists who had no faith in the Bible.

5. Those who know how the nation of Israel came into existence are aware that only the holocaust was powerful enough to move the nations of the world to vote Israel into existence out of compassion (although the move to Israel had been going on for almost a hundred years before World War II). So, to believe the Jews "caused" the fulfillment of the prophecies, one would have to believe that they somehow caused the holocaust!

If we want to explain evidence away, we can always find some way to do so. But this explanation sounds like anti-Semitic theorists who think the Jews are controlling the world! Such explanations are ludicrous and nowhere near as believable as the plain truth—that fulfilled supernatural prophecy of Israel's regathering once again shows that God speaks through the Bible.

CHAPTER 7

The Biblical Message

B efore going into several more key lines of evidence for the reality of God, we need to stop and take a few minutes to make sure we understand what message these lines of evidence validate. All lines of evidence converge toward one thing—the central biblical message about a very important word: *grace*.

Background

At the core of biblical teaching is a collision of values. On one hand are the morally good character of creator God and his abhorrence of evil. On the other hand is his love for people like us who are all guilty of wrongdoing. When these values come into conflict, God's resolution is surprising.

Before we can appreciate this resolution, we need to look at the background picture that makes sense of the whole story. Key questions lie here: Who is God? What is he like? What does he want from us? What are humans?

God

Either a God exists or not. Either he is one way or another. We have no say in this—what we believe doesn't change what God is or isn't. When it comes to questions like these, something is true and the other thing is false. Our best move would be to discover that truth and believe it *because it is true*. Unless we can know, we have no ground for believing anything other than wishful thinking.

The biblical picture of God is quite different from other pictures. Several key aspects about the God of the Bible are important to understand.

- God is *personal*. To be personal means that he has the qualities seen in personalities—the ability to form relationships, to care, to communicate, to feel, to creatively respond to what other personal beings share, and to love. Personal beings think, plan, foresee, and act accordingly. They have an opinion and a will—that is, the ability to form an intention. These things are not found in impersonal things or creatures beyond the most rudimentary level. Insects might chirp to communicate, for instance, but all their communications are alike—species can be identified by their chirp. It's totally different than human communication. Likewise, some views of god see him as impersonal, like the god of pantheism, where everything is god. In this view, god is like a force such as gravity—not someone you would talk to. But God as he is portrayed in the Bible is fully personal—he talks, reveals, cares, loves, and forms relationships.

- The biblical God is *infinite*. Unlike the gods of polytheism or animism, the God of scripture is unlimited in any way. He had no beginning, and holds all his characteristics to an infinite degree. This notion of a God who is both infinite and personal is unique to the Bible and religions like Islam that have spun off from the Bible.

- The biblical God is *morally good*. That means his nature is the definition of goodness. He cannot stand evil.

- God, according the Bible, is *loving*. He values and loves his personal creatures, like humans. Even before personal creatures like us were created, God was a God of love, because within his triune nature (of Father, Son, and Holy Spirit) there was love for one another.

- God is *just*. This is the hardest feature of God for modern people to understand or accept. Justice means God cannot simply look the other way when creatures choose to practice evil. As the sovereign leader of the universe, God is its judge. His own nature dictates that he respond fairly—matching good with reward and evil with punishment.

God has a number of other important attributes, but these alone are sufficient to understand the problem that comes up in the Bible.

The problem with the human race

The Bible teaches that the human race is in a 'fallen' state. That means we have fallen from the way God intended us to be. As freely choosing creatures, the original humans had to decide whether to follow God or to set their own course independent from him. Once the first humans turned away from God and struck out on their own, their decision immediately and permanently altered their moral nature (Genesis 3; Romans 5:12-21). Their children came out already in the same fallen state, and this has continued throughout history.

Everything on our planet, even nature, suffered from the fall of humans, because God was no longer guarding and protecting us from danger. Since the fall, God takes a hands-off policy most of the time (Romans 8:20).[26] This means that what we see in the world is abnormal and twisted compared to God's original plan.

God created the world not only in perfection but also with real freedom. Now that humans have used their freedom to turn away from God's leadership, we see the unfolding of something God abhors: evil, or "sin." In our world, only humans are evil, because only they have the capacity to choose freely. Animals cannot do morally good or evil deeds because they lack this personal dimension.

We will discuss the objections to this position later. The main point for now is that, as the Bible describes it, the central problem in our world is the evil in the human race resulting from our separation from God. The Bible places the blame for the present situation squarely on humankind, maintaining that God is guilty of nothing more than creating freedom.

The Bible teaches that all humans are guilty of evil much of the time (Romans 3:9-18; Mark 10:18). Note that this guilt is not referring to guilt *feelings*. Rather, the point is that regardless of what we feel, we are guilty of moral offenses against the character of God. Even when we do something not specifically evil, we may fail to act out of faith in God, and therefore such works fall short of God's standard of perfection (Romans 14:23). Doing the right thing isn't enough. God wants us to do the right thing and to do it for the right reasons (1 Corinthians 4:5).

The Bible goes further, warning that people are helpless in their wrongful way of life. Although we had freedom at one time, we have lost the freedom to live without sin and are now helpless to change our selfishness (John 6:44, 65; Romans 5:6, 8, 10).[27]

---

26 God is 'hands off' in the sense that he is not the direct cause of events on earth, but never in the sense that he has lost control of the situation. Jesus explained that even a sparrow could not fall from its nest "apart from the Father" (Matthew 6:29). But this doesn't mean God shoved the sparrow from its nest. It only means that by letting things happen that he could have prevented, God has 'signed off' on those things indirectly. This is called the permissive will of God, as opposed to his moral will.

27 This doesn't mean humans have no free will any longer. Our free will has been diminished, but is still present to a significant degree. That's why humans are culpable for moral wrongdoing.

We might say the Bible has a radically negative view of human-kind, at least on the moral level. At the same time, the Bible argues for the high value of human life and the beauty of human creativity because people were created in the image of God (James 3:9). Although people have fallen from their original state, this image of God is still evident—just sadly twisted. In a later chapter we'll see how our own consciousness and creative urges are clear evidence that we are exactly what the Bible says we are.

When we see the Bible declaring that all people, without exception, have this fallen nature, regardless of race, sex, or social class, we realize that this message is unusual. The idea of fallen humanity sharply diverges from what we like to think about ourselves. Yet, we should view this negative part of the Bible's message along with the positive part—the dynamic liberty possible through God's grace.

When you think about it, there must be something wrong with our race and with our world. How can anyone argue that nothing is amiss when looking at disfigured newborns, endless war and cruelty, or the sheer devastation we wreak on our environment? We will be discussing the problem of evil later, but for now, we can hopefully agree that people in our world have a negative twist at the same time they have a unique beauty.

God's response to human evil

As mentioned earlier, the biblical message centers on the concept of *grace*. Grace is very different than most religious systems, where people must work at following religious laws in order to earn the favor of God (or to work one's way up the ladder of *karma*). This notion that God requires the observance of ritual and other religious regulations in order to avoid divine judgment raises serious problems.

For one thing, it makes God seem harsh and unwelcoming. It pictures God holding up a hoop and saying, "Here, jump through this." If we do so, he says, "Do it again," and eventually, "Now keep doing it for the rest of your life." After the worshiper's death, God decides whether reward or punishment will be handed out, and to what degree.

In many cases, the laws in these religions have no apparent beneficial effect on the worshiper (for instance, reciting the same prayer over and over). It seems like the act is more for the benefit of the deity than for the benefit of the worshiper. But this is a problem also. What benefit does God need? If he is the Creator of everything, what does he gain from having his creatures go through repetitive motions?

In fact, according to this widespread view, God seems to be quite unwelcoming. A god like this is grudgingly handing out blessing and acceptance only if we earn them through hard work. He doesn't seem eager to see many people receive blessing. If he were eager, wouldn't he get rid of the hoop?

Biblical Christianity disagrees more sharply in this area than in any other. According to Jesus, "Even the Son of Man did not come to be served, but to serve, and to give his life as a ransom for many" (Mark 10:45).

According to the New Testament, Jesus' incarnation solved the problem caused by evil between God and people. Even though people stand under God's judgment, he doesn't want to see us undergo punishment for our wrongdoing (2 Peter 3:9). Therefore, Jesus came to die, suffering God's judgment in our place. The result is called "grace"—a gift from God to us. He underwent his own judgment so that we could receive eternal life as a free gift. It only remains for us to believe and accept that gift.

Many passages in the New Testament stress that God offers the gift of salvation through Christ freely to anyone who wants it. In Ephesians, Paul explained it this way: "For it is by grace you have been rescued, through faith—and this not from yourselves, it is the gift of God—not by works, so that no one can boast" (Ephesians 2:8-9).

You can see how this passage squarely denies that God has a hoop of religious laws through which we must jump. Instead, it affirms that we can do nothing except receive his gift through faith—that is, *trust* that Jesus' death and resurrection make us right with God.

Why such an ordeal?

We may wonder at this point, why would God go through all the trouble of the incarnation and the cross? If he wants to accept people, why not simply ignore the fact that they misbehave and accept everyone? When we look deeper into the nature of God, we see that such a simple answer isn't possible.

God's character is said to be just (Romans 3:26). In other words, God cannot overlook the present rebellion on earth and the actions that flow from it. His just nature requires a fair and impartial response to evil.

To understand this, suppose God responded to our evil acts the same way he did to our good acts. That would mean God makes no distinction between good and evil and, in fact, must not care. This would be no less alarming than the nasty, stingy God pictured earlier in the religious law model. An amoral God who is unconcerned about good and evil would be capable of anything and certainly would provide no answers to our dilemma. Also, if God sees atrocities on earth but assigns no blame to the human race, it implies that he feels something or someone other than humanity is to blame. Ironically, a permissive God would imply that God himself is the one who is ultimately responsible.

At the same time, the Bible teaches that God's need to judge sin is unpleasant to him because of his great love for us (2 Peter 3:9; 1 Timothy 2:4; Ezekiel 18:23; 33:11; Lamentations 3:32-33). God faced a dilemma because he loves us; yet, because he is just, punishment is required.

The radical solution

This dilemma required a radical solution. God's solution is called "atonement" or "substitution." You can see atonement and substitution pictured in the Old Testament practice of animal sacrifice: the priest would lay his hands on the head of an animal, like a goat, and confess the sins of the people. Then the goat would be killed as though the goat (which is incapable of sin and therefore, innocent) could substitute for the guilty people.

Of course, goats can't really substitute for people. This was only a picture and was, in that sense, another remarkable way of predicting in advance what Jesus was going to do. When Jesus came, John the Baptist pointed at him, saying, "Behold the lamb of God that takes away the sin of the world" (John 1:29).

So, according to the Bible, the penalty for sin must be paid, either by ourselves or by someone else. Obviously, any normal man can't bear the consequences for another because he has his own sins to pay for. Even if there were a perfect man with no sins of his own to worry about, he could only pay the price for one other man. That would be fair—one sinless person substituting for one guilty person.

God's solution was to have one person take all the punishment deserved by all people upon himself. But only an infinite person could do that. And so, God decided to come himself in the person of Jesus and undergo his own sentence on behalf of his wayward creatures. The Bible explains this solution in Romans: "He did this so that he might be just and the justifier of the one who has faith in Jesus" (Romans 3:26).

We can understand the phrase "just and the justifier" through a simple illustration.

The fair judge's son

The story is told of a judge who lived in a small town with his family. He was the fairest judge anyone could remember and had faithfully served the community for many years. One night the judge's son went out, got drunk and ran down a local girl with his car. He was caught and brought to trial before his own father. (Of course, we would never do this in our system. We would make the father refer the case to someone else—a luxury God doesn't have.)

The people in the town wondered what the judge would do. Because the judge had always been impartial, they thought he would sentence his son to a long term in prison. On the other hand, he really loved the boy. Would he overthrow his love for the sake of justice? Or would he compromise justice for the sake of love and unfairly let his son go free?

When the trial began, the courtroom was full. As the lawyers presented evidence, it became clear the boy was guilty. Finally the judge swung his gavel and said, "Guilty as charged! And the sentence is ten years in the state pen!"

A gasp went though the courtroom. Certainly, what the judge did was fair, but how could he do that to his own son? At that moment, however, the judge arose and went over to sit in the witness chair. Then he said, "But I will serve the sentence for him!"

As the judge was led away to prison, the boy walked out a free man!

Before we feel too upset about the guilty boy getting away with manslaughter in this story, remember that he represents you and me. According to the Bible, we are under a sentence of death, "for all have sinned and fall short of the glory of God" (Romans 3:23), and "The wages of sin is death, but the gift of God is eternal life in Christ Jesus our Lord" (Romans 6:23).

At the cross, God became both the *just* and the *justifier*. He showed that he was just because he did not simply ignore sin but administered the full and fair punishment. Yet he was the justifier because he had given all people the option of escaping punishment at his own expense.

How amazing to think that God was willing to go to this length to solve our problem! At the cross, God demonstrated his love in an incontestable way. He now offers you this forgiveness as a gift—the gift of grace that stands as the center post of the biblical message. "To all who believed him and accepted him, he gave the right to become children of God" (John 1:12).

What about the laws?

One might wonder why God gave us moral laws in the Bible (like the Ten Commandments) if salvation is a free gift. Paul answers this question in Romans also:

> Therefore no one will be declared righteous in [God's] sight by observing the law; rather, through the law we become conscious of sin. But now a righteousness from God, apart from law, has been made known. (Romans 3:20-21)

In other words, the religious laws in the Bible are different from those of other religions because they are not given in order to secure salvation. Instead, this passage says the law can only make us "conscious of sin." Like a mirror that shows us dirt on our face, the law shows us we fall short of the moral standards of God. The mirror cannot remove the dirt; it only shows that it is there.

Consider, for example, the law described in Deuteronomy 6:5: "Love the Lord your God with all your heart and with all your soul and with all your strength." If you take this law seriously, even allowing for a figure of speech, you realize you cannot keep it. Every one of us has broken it already and will break it many times in the future as well. That's bad news when you consider that, according to God's standard, you have to keep all the laws all the time, not just part of the time (James 2:10; Galatians 3:10).

The Old Testament law shows us our need for forgiveness. However, once we accept God's grace, we are no longer under law: "For sin shall not be your master, because you are not under law, but under grace" (Romans 6:14). Or, as Paul explains elsewhere,

> Before this faith came, we were held prisoners by the law, locked up until faith should be revealed. So the law was put in charge to lead us to Christ that we might be justified by faith. Now that faith has come, we are no longer under the supervision of the law. You are all sons of God through faith in Christ Jesus. (Galatians 3:23-26)

How different this is from other religious systems! Of course, the fact that we are not under law doesn't mean that right and wrong no longer exist for Christians. It does mean, however, that doing good cannot save a person and doing wrong will not condemn a person if that person has received the grace of Christ. This is why Paul can summarize the Christian message this way: "For we maintain that a man is justified by faith apart from observing the law" (Romans 3:28).[28]

To "receive Christ" (John 1:12) means that you consciously tell God that you accept his terms for a relationship: that you need to be forgiven, that Jesus' death is the only thing that can pay for your sins, and that you want his Spirit to come into you.

The big picture

In most religious thinking, we have a severe God who for some reason holds up a hoop for people to jump through. In the Bible, we see a picture of a God who has done all the work himself at great personal expense. God is prepared to offer forgiveness so complete that it removes all question of sin from the discussion. Then we become free to relate to God on the basis of a love relationship instead of legal performance. This relationship is available without charge to anyone who will turn to God in faith and ask. Jesus said, "Whoever comes to me I will never drive away" (John 6:37).

This, then, is the heart of biblical Christianity. Not surprisingly, people have developed different interpretations of Christianity, just like they do in every field. Some of these versions are very far indeed from what we have just detailed from scripture, so obviously, they can't all be right. In this book, we are only defending this simple biblical view centering on God's grace.

---

28 I've based much of this discussion on Romans 3 because the gospel of Christianity is clearly and fully explained there. However, this is not an isolated teaching. The same points are repeated in many other passages. If you want more study on the subject consider these passages to begin with: Luke 18:9-14; John 3:16; 5:24; 6:29; 15:1-8; Acts 16:30-31; Romans 5:20; 7:1-8:1; 1 Corinthians 6:9-11; 2 Corinthians 3:6-11; 5:19-21; Galatians 2:16; 3:24-25; Ephesians 4:32 (note completed action, "forgave"); Colossians 2:13; Hebrews 10:10-17; Jeremiah 31:31-34; Ezekiel 36:25-27.

CHAPTER 8

The Growing Case for God's Existence and Nature

Although most people believe God exists, many aren't sure why. Also, studies show that most people in the west are very unsure what God is like, or whether the God or higher power they believe in is the God of the Bible. But during the past few decades several converging lines of evidence have powerfully strengthened the case for God's existence. They also show that he must be an infinite, personal God, just like the God of the Bible, but unlike gods proposed by other religions. These new lines of evidence are so strong that even long-term agnostic and atheistic intellectuals have recently changed their position, deciding that God must exist after all.[29]

These include the world renowned atheistic philosopher, Anthony Flew, author of *There Is a God: How the World's Most Notorious Atheist Changed His Mind,* (NY: Harper One 2008);

The arguments we explain here may not specifically point to Christianity but rather to the worldview underlying Christianity—*theism*. To understand the difference between theism and other possible worldviews, I have included a chart (see next two pages) that compares the major worldview options popular in the world today. If we find that theism (the belief in an infinite, personal God) is the most credible worldview, then we can look at different theistic interpretations to determine whether one of them stands out as particularly convincing.

In this chapter, we will see arguments for theism based on observed design in the universe. The presence of design in nature implies that there must be a Creator God. Because of recent scientific discoveries, this argument has more strength today than ever before. To understand the argument, we will examine 1) what design is and how we recognize it, 2) evidence of design in the origin of life, and 3) evidence of design in the formation of the universe.

Nobel Prize winning scientist, Francis Collins, author of *The Language of God: A Scientist Presents Evidence for Belief* (NY: Simon and Schuster/Free Press 2007); and Harvard scholar, Patrick Glynn, author of *God: The Evidence: The Reconciliation of Faith and Reason in a Postsecular World* (NY: Prima Publishing 1999) among many others.

LET'S DEFINE OUR TERMS

It may seem like there are more philosophical and religious views than any normal person could comprehend. Indeed, there are more than six thousand distinct religions in the world today. But you may be surprised to find that the world's religions and philosophies tend to break down into a few major categories. Some views don't exactly fit into one of these categories, but they are a tiny fraction of the whole. Here we have the four main ways of looking at reality.

	REALITY	HUMANS
NATURALISM Atheism; Agnosticism; Existentialism	The material universe is all that exists. Reality is "one-dimensional." There is no such thing as a soul or a spirit. Everything can be explained on the basis of natural law.	Man is the chance product of a biological process of evolution. Man is entirely material. The human species will one day pass out of existence.
PANTHEISM Hinduism; Taoism; Buddhism; much New Age consciousness	Only the spiritual dimension is real; all else is illusion—*maya*. Spiritual reality—*Brahman*—is eternal, impersonal, and unknowable. Everything is a part of God (pantheism), or that God is in everything (panenthism).	Man is one with ultimate reality. Thus man is spiritual, eternal, and impersonal. Man's belief that he is an individual is an illusion.
THEISM Christianity; Islam; Judaism	An infinite, personal God exists. He created a finite, material world. Reality is both material and spiritual. The universe as we know it had a beginning and will have an end.	Humankind is the unique creation of God. People were created "in the image of God," which means that we are personal, eternal, spiritual, and biological.
ANIMISM Polytheism, thousands of tribal religions	The world is populated by spirit beings who govern what goes on. Gods and demons are the real reason behind "natural" events. Material things are real, but they have spirits associated with them and, therefore, can be interpreted spiritually.	Man is a creation of the gods like the rest of the animals. All have spirits and bodies.
POSTMODERNISM	Reality must be interpreted through our language and cultural "paradigm." Therefore, reality is "socially constructed."	Humans are nodes in a cultural reality—they are a product of their social setting. The idea that people are autonomous and free is a myth.

~ continues next page

	TRUTH	VALUES
NATURALISM Atheism; Agnosticism; Existentialism	Truth is usually understood as scientific proof. Only that which can be observed with the five senses is accepted as real or true.	No objective values or morals exist. Morals are individual preferences or socially useful behaviors. Even social morals are subject to evolution and change.
PANTHEISM Hinduism; Taoism; Buddhism; much New Age consciousness	Truth is an experience of unity with "the one-ness" of the universe. Truth is beyond all ratio-nal description. Rational thought, as it is understood in the West, cannot show us reality.	Because ultimate reality is impersonal, many pantheistic thinkers believe that there is no real distinction between good and evil. Instead, "unen-lightened" behavior is that which fails to understand essential unity.
THEISM Christianity; Islam; Judaism	Truth about God is known through revelation. Truth about the material world is gained via revelation and the five senses in conjunction with rational thought.	Moral values are the objective expression of an absolute moral being and are based on his character as the definition of what is good.
ANIMISM Polytheism, thousands of tribal religions	Truth about the natural world is discovered through the shaman figure who has visions telling him what the gods and demons are doing and how they feel.	Moral values take the form of taboos; things that irritate or anger various spirits. These taboos are different from the idea of "good and evil" because it is just as important to avoid irritating evil spirits as good ones. Often, tribes or races have a special relationship with some gods who protect them and can punish them.
POSTMODERNISM	Truths are mental constructs meaningful to individuals within a particular cultural paradigm. They do not apply to other paradigms. Truth is relative to one's culture.	Values are part of our social paradigms as well. Tolerances, freedom of expression, inclusion, and avoiding any claim to have the answers are the main universal values.

What is design, and how do we recognize it?

Imagine you are climbing in a mountain range, and come across a cliff face with a large, smooth area where lines of scratches in strange shapes strike you as some kind of human engraving. You can't make out what the script is, but the arrangement of the scratches in lines and the general structure seem to be man-made, not naturally occurring. You feel it resembles some kind of script. Of course, there are other alternatives. The cliff face is marred and scratched in many places, so this could just be an accidental resemblance to a human language.

You're not an archeologist, so you report the find to the local university, and then lead a team of interested scientists back up to photograph the marks and make a casting. They declare that this must be very archaic, because none of them have seen the script before. But later, your sense that it's a language proves correct. The scientists use computer technology to analyze the sequence of characters and are able to decode the script. They learn that it tells the story of a chief of an area village who was buried nearby. Following the landmarks in the inscription, they actually find the burial site and the chief's remains.

Once they decoded the characters, the earlier thought—that the scratches could have been made naturally—is no longer possible. As soon as you realize the characters are a code that refers to something outside the scratches themselves, you know it has to be the result of intelligent design. Only intelligent beings like humans are capable of creating such specified complex codes referring to something external to themselves. This removes all doubt; there is *no chance* that such a script could come about by undirected natural means.

This story points to a truth we all intuitively sense. The world is full of complexity and much of it occurs naturally. But once we find complexity that refers to some external pattern or purpose (like this example of a script), it can come from no source other than intelligent and purposeful design.

Now, by analogy, we can look at two key areas where the same principle applies far more clearly than it would with this story.

The origin of life

At one time, cells were believed to be relatively simple containers of a jelly-like material called protoplasm. Only during the past few decades has science finally come to understand the staggering complexity in even the simplest cell. Now we realize this system has unmistakable design and must have had a high level of design even before any type of evolution would have been possible.

At the center of the cell is DNA. Now that science has decoded DNA we know that each strand of DNA contains vast quantities of information that give instructions for the assembly of complicated protein molecules that make up the cell. So, the code in DNA refers to a reality outside itself—just like the language in our story, but far more complex. Renowned computer programmer, Bill Gates, said that the information processing capabilities of DNA are "like a computer program but far, far more advanced than any software ever created."[30]

We now know that this universal code of life is always present and is no less complex in any form of life. Proteins never assemble themselves in any other way than through this astonishing assembly and coding system.

And this isn't all. In addition to the very elaborate coding system in DNA, living organisms also employ an even more complex assembly system for putting the instructions found in DNA into effect. These organelles and very complex enzymes are a system made up of multiple machines all working together like a factory.

Here's the rub: on one hand, DNA cannot construct proteins without the assembly machinery; but on the other hand the assembly machinery doesn't know what to do without DNA. Both depend on each other for their roles. Here again then, we have unquestionable

---

30   Bill Gates, *The Road Ahead*, (NY: Penguin Books, 1996) 188.

need for intelligence. These two systems are like computer software and hardware. Both are needed and they work together—something that never happens apart from design.

Here is a crucial point to remember: natural selection cannot be invoked to explain this system. Natural selection only works *after* self-replication is in place. On the question of how these systems came into being in the first place, natural selection offers no explanation.

Naturalists are struggling to find a way around this dilemma, proposing that perhaps compounds like RNA (which resembles half a strand of DNA) might replicate themselves without help from the usual assembly machinery like that in cells. The problems with this claim are huge. Where a complex polymer like RNA came from is never explained. Why a ribose-based compound that is unstable in water would form in the first place, or last long enough to replicate, is never explained. So far, RNA has never come anywhere near to replicating itself without relying on the other assembly machinery in the cell. This is true even though researchers bring together high concentrations of all necessary compounds and catalysts in scenarios that never could have happened on the pre-biotic earth.[31]

All life as we know it contains this amazing system for self replication, except for some parasitic viruses that use other organisms' systems. So, in a word, this is how living organisms replicate and anyone who suggests some imaginary alternative is speculating in an area of blind faith without any observable backing. With the formation of original life (what scientists call abiogenesis), we have an unmistakable case of intelligent, purposeful design.

---

31 See a convincing but technical refutation of recent exaggerated claims that RNA has self-replicated in Stephen C. Meyer and Paul A. Nelson, "Can the Origin of the Genetic Code Be Explained by Direct RNA Templating?" *Biocomplexity* Vol. 2011, #2.

The origin of the universe

Only a few decades back, naturalists still believed the universe might be eternal. Then, when Hubble discovered that the universe is expanding, they supposed it could be oscillating in and out for eternity. We don't hear that anymore. The oscillating universe theory has been laid to rest for a host of reasons. Many naturalistic scientists and mathematicians hated the idea that the universe has a beginning for one obvious reason—it points to a creator. How could a universe as vast as ours come out of a speck of near nothing?

At the same time, mainly during the past couple of decades, a host of other mysterious findings have come to light that now make creation nearly certain in the minds of many scientists. This new field of study goes under the heading of "fine tuning."

Fine tuning

During the past few decades, science has become increasingly aware that our universe, with its ability to sustain life, is astonishingly improbable. Only recently have physicists come to realize that over twenty variables involving physical forces, particles, events, and ratios between these have to be exactly what they are within an amazingly narrow window in order to sustain life. The chances that this situation would come to pass accidentally are so astronomically unlikely that it becomes statistically impossible.

Agnostic astrophysicist, Paul Davies, is a world-renowned expert and the author of several books on this subject. He explains:

> If the initial explosion of the big bang had differed in strength by as little as 1 part in 10^{60}, the universe would have either quickly collapsed back on itself, or expanded too rapidly for stars to form. In either case, life would be impossible.[32]

---

32 Paul Davies, *The Accidental Universe*, (Cambridge: Cambridge University Press, 1982) 90-91.

And,

> Calculations by Brandon Carter show that if gravity had been
> stronger or weaker by 1 part in 10^{40}, then life-sustaining stars
> like the sun could not exist. This would most likely make life
> impossible.[33]

What do these statements mean? They are saying that key
components of our universe are so unlikely that they could never
happen by chance. Here is an illustration from physicist, Robin
Collins, to explain what it means to hit a lucky draw when you have
only 1 chance in 10^{37}:

> Cover the entire North American continent in dimes all the
> way up to the moon, a height of about 239,000 miles (In com-
> parison, the money to pay for the U.S. federal government
> debt would cover one square mile less than two feet deep with
> dimes.). Next, pile dimes from here to the moon on a billion
> other continents the same size as North America. Paint one
> dime red and mix it into the billions of piles of dimes. Blind-
> fold a friend and ask him to pick out one dime. The odds that
> he will pick the red dime are one in 10^{37}.[34]

How likely is that? Not very, but there's a problem. Any dime you
drew out would be equally improbable—one chance in 10^{37}—so,
why marvel that this one came out? Thus, naturalists discredit any
argument from improbability.

But this is only the beginning. Now, suppose you put all these
trillions of dimes in a giant cosmic hopper where you can spin it
for good mixing. Then, instead of putting one red dime in, you put
in twenty red dimes. Then, after spinning the hopper to mix well,
a blindfolded man reaches in and draws out one dime. It's red. But
wait. You're not done. Now, spin the hopper again to mix thoroughly

33 Paul Davies, *Superforce: The Search for a Grand Unified Theory of Nature,* (New York:
Simon and Schuster, 1984) 242.

34 http://www.godandscience.org/apologetics/designun.html.

and have the blindfolded man reach in again. Again, he draws out a red dime!

This process would have to be repeated twenty times, and the man would have to draw out twenty red dimes, *and zero normal dimes*. No. That isn't going to happen. This is way beyond what mathematicians call a statistical impossibility. And yet drawing twenty sequential red dimes out of a batch this large is far *more likely* than what we see in the fine tuning of the universe. Fine tuning isn't just one improbability, but a confluence of dozens of the most extreme improbabilities, mostly unrelated to one another.

When reading about fine tuning, you will notice something interesting: although scientists differ on how to interpret fine tuning (especially whether it points to an intelligent creator), they do *not* disagree significantly about the numbers. Accessing the actual math involved in fine tuning is beyond the reach of most of us. However, we can rest assured that with the level of hostility seen between naturalists and theistic explanations, they would definitely mention their disagreement if they had any. Instead, they only debate what it means, not the fact of fine tuning.[35]

What would naturalists say?

Instead of challenging the reality of fine tuning, non-theistic scientists have brought forward an explanation they call "the multiverse theory." According to this theory, our universe is just one of billions or trillions of other invisible universes. Each one is different and most of them wouldn't support life. But, if there are perhaps an infinite number of other universes, eventually one like this one is likely to happen!

---

35 Recently, a few atheists have brought forward arguments to the effect that the universe is not finely tuned, because some areas are not suitable to life. The thought seems to be that unless every part of the universe is finely tuned for life, none of it is. Others appear not to understand the argument, simply claiming that other kinds of life would exist if the universe was different. But what kind of life is supposed to exist in a universe made up of nothing but hydrogen, or nothing but black holes, or that has collapsed back onto itself? The consequences of variance in the finely tuned variables do not allow for *any* kind of life.

It may seem strange that people are willing to believe in trillions of other universes that they can neither observe nor measure. But there's a reason. Again, agnostic physicist, Paul Davies, comes right out and admits why the multiverse theory is appealing:

> Scientists have long been aware that the universe seems strangely suited to life, but they mostly chose to ignore it. It was an embarrassment—it looked too much like the work of a Cosmic Designer... Today the mood has changed. What made a difference was the idea of a multiverse, which offers the opportunity to explain the weird bio-friendliness of the universe as a straightforward selection effect, *without invoking divine providence.*[36]

This is an amazingly honest admission. But ask yourself: is it really easier to believe in trillions of invisible universes than to believe in an intelligent creator? Why? Remember, the concept of a multiverse didn't arise based on any discovery of science or mathematical calculation. It arose for one reason—to explain away the appearance of design in the universe, as Davies admits in the previous quotation.

What would theists say?

Theists look at the wonders in fine tuning and abiogenesis with a satisfied smile. This is exactly the kind of thing you would expect from an infinite, personal creator. Hebrews 11:3 says, "By faith we understand that the worlds were prepared by the word of God, so that what is seen was not made out of things which are visible." This is exactly what science tells us happened with the universe. Meanwhile, the appearance of sophisticated coding systems that are externally referential, like DNA, are not surprising either. Languages and codes are always created by beings with great intelligence.

---

36 Emphasis mine. Paul Davies, *Goldilocks Engima: Why Is the Universe Just Right for Life?* (NY: Houghton Mifflin Harcourt, 2008) 151.

Notice that an impersonal picture of God like that in pantheism (where God is in everything) can't explain the incredible design we see. Only a being who could think, plan, and then purposefully carry out that plan could explain the facts. Neither could the finite nature spirits in animistic religion explain creation. These fallible spirit beings were themselves created, according to the folklore.

A God who might be sufficient to account for the universe we see and for the complexity of life would have to pre-date the universe itself; in all likelihood he would have to be infinite and without beginning. He would be "from everlasting to everlasting" (Psalms 41:13).

Isn't it amazing that the only religions in the world today that advance an infinite, personal God are Islam, Judaism, and Christianity? All three go straight back to one amazing book—the Bible.

The big picture

If we put some dynamite under a pile of bricks and blew it up, how likely is it that when the bricks fell to earth again, they would fall in the shape of the Taj Mahal? Somehow we intuitively know this will never happen. Although the system contains sufficient energy and the correct building blocks to build the Taj Mahal, something is missing. Even if we repeated the experiment millions of times over, it would never result in the Taj Mahal or any other kind of building. That's just not how random things work.

Suppose that after one of our blasts, we found one brick lying atop another. Someone might say, "Look! This shows it's possible!"[37] No, it doesn't. Although the building blocks and sufficient energy are present, the energy must be channeled in the very precise ways required to produce a complex design.

---

37 One brick on top of another is a good analogy for those who claim the Miller-Urey experiment shows that abiogenesis is possible because a glass bell produced amino acids. But amino acids are very simple compounds that are no closer to functioning protein than a couple of bricks would be to the Taj Mahal.

Of course, the more complex the design, the more difficult it is to believe it happened by accident and living organisms are much more complex than the Taj Mahal. The fine tuning of the universe is so extreme that it's very difficult to even understand. Wouldn't it be more sensible to believe that someone acting with intelligence and purpose has arranged things this way?

I'm not suggesting that this argument proves that a personal God exists. But it does strongly suggest that he exists and has created our universe. In fact, the more you think about it, the more likely you are to realize that the reality of a personal creator God is far more likely than any other explanation for the amazing design in our world. That is a key reason that world renowned atheistic philosopher, Anthony Flew, changed his view to belief in God. He explains:

> I think the most impressive arguments for God's existence are those that are supported by recent scientific discoveries... the argument to Intelligent Design is enormously stronger than it was when I first met it.[38]

---

38 Anthony Flew and Gary Habermas, "My Pilgrimage from Atheism to Theism: A Discussion Between Antony Flew and Gary Habermas," *Philosohia Christi* 6. 2 (2004): 200. Flew, now deceased, never believed in Jesus or the Bible as far as we know.

CHAPTER 9

God Evident Through Consciousness

My most basic and obvious observation is that "I am me." I have been "me" my whole life, even though every molecule in my body is probably different than what I started with. I remember events before kindergarten, but it was still the same "me" as today. I have a physical body and a brain, but the "me" in there is different than the physical parts. Inwardly, every one of us perceives an array of things that say unmistakably that we have consciousness, that we have minds, and that we are selves.

Take a minute to think carefully about the nature of consciousness, personhood, and the mind:

- **Inside is your "mind's eye:"** You have an ability to see things without seeing them, whether real scenes you've seen before, or completely imaginary scenes you create out of nothing.

- **Symbolic language:** Not barking, screeching, or wailing an emotion due to some stimulus (although we can do this too), but ideas encoded into elaborate sound sequences that can be received and decoded by another with a high degree of accuracy. Shapes on paper can describe the sound sequence in letters for reading. Our language is not just simple requests or warnings; we commonly exchange elaborate abstract concepts (like this book) with other humans. People without hearing learn to speak with finger and hand motions. Those without sight can read using the sense of feel.

- **Creativity and artistic appreciation:** As humans, we find ourselves enchanted by music, art, cinema, and other types of aesthetic creations to the extent that we often spend hours every day dwelling on them. How strange that only humans engage in this type of activity, which creates neither food nor shelter, and might actually work against survival in many situations. Even the most primitive peoples are no different than the most modern in this regard.

- **Morality:** In spite of some people's efforts to deny it, we all have an undeniable awareness that some things are just plain wrong. We may not agree on moral questions, but everyone uses moral thinking and knows moral motions within. The evidence is strong that people's sense of what is moral derives from their culture. But here we are not referring to the *content* of moral norms, but the *existence* of a moral sense itself.[39] This is exclusively human, and all humans know that animals are not capable of moral or immoral behavior, because they are instinctual rather than free-choosing moral agents.

- **Love:** Again, some try to deny it, but when we are honest with ourselves, we know that love is something special. It is neither

---

39 From a biblical point of view, humans' disagreement over what is morally right or wrong is the result of our fallen state, which caused humans to launch off into independent views on such questions. This is what Genesis means when it refers to "the tree of the knowledge of good and evil" (Genesis 2:17). But the presence of a moral sense is something built into humans as part of their nature as free choosing moral agents.

the breeding instinct nor the herding instinct, but a uniquely deep experience that remains elusive in a fallen world.

- **Decision making:** Every one of us knows what it is to weigh evidence, consider alternatives, compare costs and benefits, and then to make a decision (not that we always make decisions this carefully). Weighing alternatives, judging the relative validity of arguments—these require unfettered freedom. If we weren't able to freely analyze, sift, and appraise information before making a decision, we wouldn't really be making rational decisions. None of our conclusions could be trusted. But most people are shocked to learn what Harvard mind science expert, Leonid Perlovsky says: "Most contemporary philosophers and scientists do not believe that free will exists."[40] We'll see why this is below—all the features on this list are incompatible with naturalism.

When we consider these obvious traits found in humans, and connect the dots on how they came into being, they end up pointing directly to the existence of an infinite, personal creator God.

Where you begin determines where you end up

Everyone has to begin somewhere in their thinking. You might observe "I'm here, I see a world and I think it's real." That's a beginning point. Then you would have to add other assumptions along the way to any coherent worldview. You might conclude that things that

---

40 He goes on, "The reconciliation of scientific causality and free will remains an unsolved problem.... Let me repeat the fact that most scientists do not believe in free will." Don't believe claims that science has shown how thinking or choice works. Perlovsky (himself a naturalist) describes the true current state of mind science: "Physical biology has explained the molecular foundations of life, DNA and proteins. Cognitive science has explained many mental processes in terms of material processes in the brain. Yet... cognitive science is only approaching some of the foundations of perception and simplest actions.... It is not a tautology that we have no idea of nearly 99% of our mind's functioning." Leonid Perlovsky, "Free Will and Advances in Cognitive Science," 2010 1, 3, 6.

make sense are likely true, while contradictory things are not true. You might decide that loving actions are better than violent actions.

As you reach more conclusions during the course of life, it's important to make sure your conclusions line up with your beginning assumptions. Otherwise, you're not only believing and behaving inconsistently; you could be guilty of hypocrisy. Any worldview that contradicts its own beginning point fails the test of internal consistency and must be false.

People holding such views are "talking out of both sides of their mouths," as the saying goes. Internal inconsistency means a person is either mistaken or dishonest. Suppose I have a friend who claims gravity has no effect on him, yet I notice he always wears a parachute when flying. I put the question, "So, I thought you aren't subject to gravity?"

"That's right," he replies.

"Then, what's with the parachute?"

"Oh... Yeah, I just wear this," he shrugs.

What's wrong with this picture? This could happen in many areas. Suppose your spouse says she loves you, but wants to have an affair with another man. She either doesn't know what love means, or she's lying. Let's look at another illustration to see how this applies to understanding life.

Entering Canada

Imagine a lady and a man riding in a railway coach. Coming into a station and glancing from the window, they see numerous white stones scattered about on a hillside near the train in a pattern resembling these letters: THE CANADIAN RAILWAY WELCOMES YOU TO CANADA.

The lady observes that it must have taken a lot of work to arrange the stones in that pattern, but the man disagrees, saying he sees no proof that any work was expended on the arrangement. After all, similar stones are present on other parts of the hill, and because they are on a slope they might roll down periodically. How could anyone know the stones didn't just accidentally roll into this curious arrangement?

At this point, the lady may feel that the man is being credulous and irrational, but, technically speaking, she has to admit she can't prove (from where they are sitting) that anyone arranged the rocks this way. Still, she feels her explanation is easier to believe than the man's.

(So far, this is an argument from design like that in the previous chapter. Now observe a further step we can take based on our beginning points.)

A few minutes later, the man suggests they should get out at the station and exchange their U.S. currency for Canadian money.

The lady looks up with narrowed eyes. "What makes you think we should do that?"

The man points to the rocks on the hill, "Can't you read? It says we are entering Canada!"

At this point, whether he realizes it or not, the man demonstrates that he, too, believes the arrangement of the stones is no accident. The fact that he draws conclusions about the world based on the arrangement of the stones is totally inconsistent with his earlier claim that they had fallen into that pattern by accident. He can't possibly believe that the stones mean he is entering Canada unless he, too, thinks the stones were placed in this arrangement by a purposeful being in order to communicate something. (Notice again how the complexity of the stone arrangement refers to something outside itself—the Canadian border—a sure sign of intelligent design.)[41]

Yes, if the stones fell accidentally into this arrangement, it could also be an accident that it happened near the Canadian border. But the point here isn't one of probability. The man draws his conclusion that they are at the border *based on the arrangement of the rocks.* This

---

41 This illustration is adapted from a similar illustration by Richard Taylor, cited in John Hick, *Arguments for the Existence of God* (New York: Herder and Herder, 1971), 23-24. See also J. P. Moreland, *Scaling the Secular City,* pp. 77-103.

would not be possible or rational unless the rocks were intentionally and purposefully arranged.

Applying the analogy

In one area after another, we will find that naturalism is just like the man in this story—claiming one beginning point, but reaching conclusions that could only come from a different starting point.

Belief in freedom

Consider this claim from atheist, Stephen Hawking: "The molecular basis of biology shows that biological processes are governed by the laws of physics and chemistry and therefore are as determined as the orbits of the planets... so it seems that we are no more than biological machines and that free will is just an illusion."[42] He's right. Material objects are incapable of freedom. They behave as the laws of physics dictate.

Yet most of us, including naturalists, act and think in ways that imply we believe people are free in their choices. For instance, when we criticize rapists or tyrants for doing terrible things, we imply that they are able to freely choose to do differently. Otherwise, why criticize them for doing only what they are compelled to do in a deterministic system? When we feel such outrage, it shows that we believe people are making free choices and that they (and ourselves) are not marionettes on strings.

The same is true any time we try to persuade someone. If Hawking really believed what he said above, why would he write a book designed to persuade people to think differently? According to his own statement, their thinking is as fixed as the orbits of planets. The fact that he thinks people can be persuaded to change their minds implies that he really believes they have free choice, even though his

---

42   Stephen Hawking, and Leonard Mlodinow, *The Grand Design*, (NY: Bantam, 2010) 32.

worldview cannot account for freedom. He is no different than the man on the train suggesting they change their currency.

Anyone who acts as though people are free-choosing beings, rather than determined ones, needs to account for why we would have such freedom. The idea that we are free contradicts key assumptions of both naturalism and postmodernism (which holds that we are determined by our culture and language rather than by physics). If we believe in freedom, we also must believe in a creator God. Let's see why this is so.

Matter + energy + chance ≠ freedom

When you pour vinegar over baking soda, it foams. It's a physical event—a chemical reaction. There is no freedom involved. The chemicals don't "decide" to react this way, they do precisely what the laws of nature prescribe under those circumstances. Each and every time we put the same chemicals together under the same conditions, they will behave *exactly* the same way.

Likewise, according to the naturalistic worldview, our thought processes are nothing but chemical reactions and electrical impulses in our neurons. Such reactions are much more complicated than soda and vinegar, but they are also determined by the same conditions and laws of physics and chemistry. If this is so, then, according to naturalists, what we perceive as free thinking is actually caused by the environment and is beyond our ability to control. But if our thought processes are not free, then any naturalist who treats others as though they were free is being inconsistent, like the man on the train. When an atheist goes on to try to persuade or change someone's thinking, he gives himself away. His worldview is so untenable he can't be consistent with it. Actions speak louder than words.

By contrast, as theists, we argue that the basis for real freedom is the eternally free and sovereignly choosing Creator God who has made humans in his image. Our thoughts may involve chemical reactions, but we also have an immaterial mind, or a soul, which lies outside physical law. Our will can govern our thoughts and make decisions when we want it to. Our thoughts have meaning and importance because they are substantially free, and this is perfectly consistent with a personal creator.[43]

Belief in morality

We find the same sort of inconsistency whenever someone affirms such a thing as morality, while denying a Creator God. If we say there is such a thing as moral right and wrong, we are implying that there must be a universal and personal basis for morals. A minute of thought will show why this is so.

Is it morally wrong to sexually abuse three-year-old girls? Is the rightness or wrongness of such an act purely a personal choice, or is there a universal moral standard at stake? If such a moral norm is universal and lies beyond individual choice, then such actions are wrong whether the perpetrator thinks so or not. However, such a universal moral norm must have a universal basis.

Naturalists who don't believe in God think the universe is nothing more than particles and energy. But such a view cannot teach us that child abuse is wrong, or that human life matters. Quite the contrary. Imagine a breeze catching a piece of paper and blowing it off a table onto the floor. Is that event morally good or evil? Obviously, it is neither. This is nothing but matter and energy following natural law. It can't be moral. This is why a materialistic, naturalistic view of the world cannot result in objective moral norms of any kind.

Confidence in rationality

Again, if the universe is a random collection of matter and energy, as

---

43   Today naturalists try to argue that quantum theory has provided an explanation for how people can be free in a material universe. However, it has only demonstrated randomness and uncertainty, not freedom in the sense of free choice. Such freedom requires *intent*, which quantum physics do not explain. Besides this, the mechanisms of thought and brain function are not subatomic. They are molecular reactions governed by the same principles of chemistry and physics that govern other mechanistic reactions in nature. Only a non-material soul can account for true freedom as seen in consciousness.

naturalists claim, why would we assume that it makes rational sense? And yet, any time we use our reasoning ability to draw conclusions or to look at patterns in the universe, trying to discover truth (such as scientific laws), we are affirming by our actions that we already believe the universe has a rational basis. Otherwise, why would we think rational analysis would tell us anything about it?

Rational analysis of our world only makes sense if we assume the world itself makes rational sense in the first place. Somehow, there must be a connection between our rationality and the structure of the universe. But we have no reason to believe the universe makes sense unless we also believe it came from a rational source and is, in fact, reasonable in its very makeup.

When people, including naturalists, use their reason to interpret the world, they show by their actions that they believe humans have minds that are free and undetermined. Otherwise a person would not really be thinking. He would only be responding to stimuli, like leaves wiggling in the wind. Naturalists who deny free will end up in the ludicrous position of using their minds to argue that they have no minds. How can this be an honest position?

Anyone who trusts that thoughts are telling him something about reality should admit the world was created by a rational being who imbued us with the ability to think. Otherwise, they are just like the skeptical man on the train wanting to change their currency to Canadian. They show by their actions that they believe the rocks (like their minds) are not random, but contain an orderly and rational arrangement.

So, confidence in reason is consistent with theism, not with naturalism. The ability to reason reliably requires freedom and the source of such freedom is the free God who imbued us with non-material souls that are not subject to physical law. Confidence in reason also requires that at some level our environment is reasonable. This reasonable and orderly basis to the universe is none other than the reasoning and personal One who created all, and is himself the ground of all being.

Theists don't believe reason is sufficient to tell us everything. Many things lie beyond our ability to perceive or comprehend with unaided reason (and some of these things can be known through revelation). When we do use reason as theists, we are not being self-contradictory or hypocritical, and that's important.

The big picture

This chapter has been more complicated, but hopefully you can see the point: in one area after another we find it impossible to act consistently with worldviews that deny an infinite, personal, creator God. Such worldviews fail the test of internal consistency and should be rejected by honest thinkers. Why is theism the only worldview that avoids such internal contradiction? It's because the real world really is the result of creation. Because reality is what it is, inconsistency is unavoidable whenever we try to think and behave as though it all happened apart from God. But when we admit God is real, everything falls into place with perfect consistency.

Notice the point here isn't just that belief in God will help you think better or to be more consistent in your views. The point is that theism is true.

Why can't we make an aircraft shaped like a box? It's because aircraft have to interact with the real world in a way that results in flight. So the shape of a wing is not arbitrary. It has to be shaped that way, because in the real world, the curve of the wing results in lift. Wings work because they are properly designed for the real world.

Likewise, our minds work when we align them with reality: the fact that a personal, moral, and rational God has indeed created us and our world.

Consider this comment by Albert Einstein, as he discussed how the progress of science depends on scientists freely trying different ideas to explain what they see:

> The liberty of choice [in applying new ideas], however, is of a special kind; it is not in any way similar to the liberty of a

writer of fiction. Rather it is similar to that of a man engaged in solving a well designed word puzzle. He may, it is true, propose any word as the solution; but, there is only one word which really solves the puzzle in all its forms. It is an outcome of faith that nature—as she is perceptible to our five senses— takes the character of such a well formulated puzzle. The successes reaped up to now by science do, it is true, give a certain encouragement for this faith....[44]

In this statement, Einstein (who was not a theist, but did believe in some higher power) agrees with the point of this chapter. He compares the universe to a word puzzle.

Now think about what assumptions would be required in order to solve this puzzle.

1. First, before even trying to solve it, you would have to believe that it is a crossword puzzle, not just random marks on a page. This is just like needing to know the universe is reasonable.

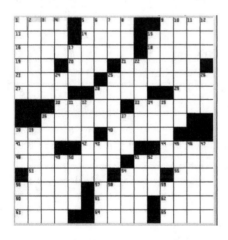

2. Therefore, if this is a crossword puzzle, some thinking, planning being composed it. Otherwise, you have no reason to think words would fit and make it work out.

3. Once you do solve it, the fact that it works confirms the original assumptions, 1 and 2. This is why Einstein says scientific progress

---

44 Albert Einstein, "General Consideration Concerning the Method of Science" in *The Journal of the Franklin Institute* (221, 3, 1936).

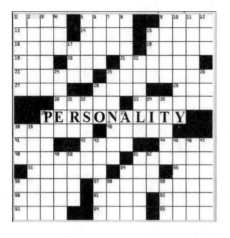

tends to confirm faith in order.

Here, you can see visually why approaching the world reasonably implies creation. But this becomes even clearer when you add the first word to the puzzle, a big word that lies right in the center, and which cannot be otherwise, you also determine how the rest of the puzzle must work.

The things we listed at the beginning of this chapter—our certain sense that "I am me," that I can see and reason, that I am making free decisions, that I am a moral being, a creative being—these observations dictate how the rest of the puzzle works.

If we can't believe these ultimately clear observations about ourselves, we can't believe anything we perceive. Yet, all of these features of personhood, like the puzzle itself, require a planning, purposeful creator. This whole picture is just like the rocks on the hillside telling us we are about to enter Canada.

Our purposeful creator: not a vague force that could never account for personhood because it lacks personhood itself, but a true, personal being—he is the one we need to meet and get to know if we want to live life to the full.

CHAPTER 10

Meeting God

If you came to this book to explore the possibilities of faith, you may by now feel interested in meeting God in a personal and direct way. Although you may still have doubts and unclear areas, you reach a point where further progress is impossible without taking action.

Maybe you're like the person in our earlier story about the three-hour party in Chapter 1. As you stand next to the closed door that supposedly offers healing, your new acquaintance tries to show you this is not a scam or something false. He claims to have been on the other side of the door and shows you pictures of what is there (of course, those pictures could be from anywhere). He is able to give plausible explanations for why they have a cure for the disease killing everyone (but he could be making it up).

Perhaps he also takes a polygraph as evidence that he is telling the truth (but polygraphs can err, and it may only show that he *thinks* he's telling the truth). He introduces you to a string of others who say they earlier went through the door, got healed, and came back now feeling awesome. They seem like normal well-adjusted and friendly people (but they could all be working together in a conspiracy, or they may be mistaken). He could show you a technical article that seems plausible (but you don't fully understand it).

This conversation could go on forever, and there would always be room for doubt. When do you reach the point where it makes sense to open the door and see for yourself if anything is there? Part of the answer to this question would depend on how risky it is to open the door. If there is little or no risk, you might as well open the door and see what's in there. Maybe this is where you are at this moment.

In Revelation 3:20, Jesus says, "Here I am! I stand at the door and knock. If anyone hears my voice and opens the door, I will come in and eat with him, and he with me." (Dining was considered a very personal kind of fellowship in that day.) Even if you have been involved in church, you still need to take Christ up on this offer. This passage isn't about church membership. Rather, Jesus is inviting you into personal fellowship with him.

Will you open that door and let Jesus enter your life right now? This is the best way to continue exploring God. You may not understand everything, and you may have doubts or reservations. If you do have doubts, simply tell that to God and ask for confirmation that he has entered your life. You should admit that you fall short of God's standards, and that you are going to trust the Jesus' death to pay for your sins so that God can forgive you.

What will happen if you open that door? That depends. Some people report a clear sense that something has changed, and they can feel the love of God. Others don't have any distinct experience at first. If you're like this, only during the weeks that follow does the presence of God in your life become more and more noticeable as you begin to grow spiritually. Allow some time for the Holy Spirit to reveal himself in your life.

Building a relationship

If you call out to God to accept his offer, he will answer. Once you open the door of your heart to Jesus, the next step is to get to know him. You should consider following up with God in several ways.

Scripture

God has given us the Bible as revelation of himself. Start reading in the New Testament. John is an excellent first book to read; so is Romans. The Old Testament is harder to read, especially the historical and prophetic books. If you want to read in the Old Testament, try Psalms or Proverbs for starters.

For people in relationship with God, the Bible is like food. As with physical food, if you don't eat, you'll be malnourished. Peter said: "Like newborn babes, long for the pure milk of the word, that by it you may grow in respect to salvation" (1 Peter 2:2). Jesus also taught that the Bible is essential for growth: "If you abide in my word, then you are truly disciples of mine; and you shall know the truth, and the truth shall make you free" (John 8:31-3).

If you have doubts, the Bible will also help you deal with those. The more you understand the answers given in Scripture, the more your faith will grow. "Faith comes from hearing the message, and the message is heard through the word of Christ" (Romans 10:17). Come to the text of the Bible expecting to connect with God.

Fellowship

One of the most important things you can do is to find a Bible study group or partner. If you know someone who is into following Jesus, ask for help.

Considering how many strange groups are around today under the name "Christian," you need to be careful when making the choice of a Christian fellowship or church. In this book, I have consistently stressed that only the biblical version of Christianity commends itself. The Bible has both reliable answers and built-in credibility. But a group based primarily on tradition or people's visions lacks this credibility and could even be dangerous. As a new believer, you need help getting started in Bible study, and a Bible study group is a good place to start.

Since some groups have little to do with biblical Christianity, you should make every effort to distinguish between those groups that are faithful to the message of the Bible and those that are not. For instance, any church that sees no need for regular Bible study is not trustworthy. Why would a church based on the Bible not study the Bible? One reason is that some modern church leaders have forsaken belief in the Bible and are actually embarrassed by the supernatural. They see the Bible as a human creation, no more enlightening than other holy books. Such leaders cannot help you understand the true God of the Bible.

Many authoritarian groups in operation today call for unconditional obedience to church authority. You should carefully avoid this kind of group because they are elevating human authority to the same level as the Bible. You should avoid groups that are highly legalistic, bossy, or restrictive. Ask around until you find a group that is growing in love and the grace of God. Jesus said the fruit teachers bear would show whether or not they are trustworthy. Foremost among these fruits is a real caring love (Galatians 5:22; John 13:34).

If you find a group of sincere Christians engaged in learning and living the truths of scripture, God will be able to give you life-changing insight.[45] In healthy groups like these, you will be able to make friends at a level you've never known before.

Prayer: talking to God

Opening the door to Jesus is the beginning of a relationship, and relationships can't go far without personal communication. You need to begin talking to God. When praying, you can address God as Lord and friend (Matthew 6:7-8; John 15:14-15). Don't worry about what to say. Just speak to God from the heart about the things you are going through and the way you feel. You can share with God anything

---

45   One of the easiest and most reliable ways to find a good Bible study group in most American and European cities is to contact a parachurch organization. Navigators, Inter-Varsity Christian Fellowship, Youth for Christ, and Campus Crusade for Christ are examples of student-oriented parachurch groups based in most metropolitan areas. Ask one of these groups where a good church or Bible study group is in your area. They will know which churches and fellowships are faithful to Scripture.

bothering you (Philippians 4:6-7). You can ask him questions, which he may answer on the spot (usually by giving you inner insight), or during the days to follow.

Safety

Finally, you need to realize how secure you are with God. You need never fear that you will offend God and cause him to withdraw from you. Romans 8:1 says: "Therefore, there is now no condemnation for those who are in Christ Jesus," and in John 6:37 Jesus said, "Whoever comes to me I will never drive away." Jesus' death is completely sufficient and you will never exhaust his forgiveness, so you are secure in your relationship with God even if you fall into sin. Like a loving father who may be distressed if his children do wrong, God may be grieved at times, but he will not withdraw. His patience is infinite. Never listen to the accusing voice of the enemy saying that God is sick of you.

As you grow spiritually, you will begin to notice evidences of the presence of the Holy Spirit in your life, including a new outlook on life and a growing hunger for the Bible and Christian fellowship. Your own relationship with God will become more rewarding and tangible. Many Christians find they have a new sensitivity to right and wrong. Christians often find themselves becoming uncomfortable with some activities they used to do with no problem. And usually, Christians discover a growing desire to see others meet Christ.

God will reassure you in various ways as you position yourself to receive blessings from him. As you continue to grow spiritually, you will eventually reach the place where you are as sure of Christ's presence with you as you are of the presence of your other friends.

CHAPTER 11

For Further Reading: Objections to the Biblical Worldview

I f you have areas of tension in your thinking that challenge the truthfulness of Jesus, this chapter might help. The case for theism, and specifically biblical theism, is strong. The prospect of establishing a relationship with God based on the work of Jesus is also very attractive, but only if his message is real and true. That's the main point: is the biblical message true because it comes from God? Or is it just a book with some unusual features?

While we have seen solid confirming evidence that the Bible comes from God, people have problems with Jesus, and even more so with the traditional church. Some feel the Bible is itself contradictory and inconsistent at certain points. This chapter looks at some of the main lines of argument used to discredit Jesus and the Bible.

The following is a brief outline of the questions addressed:

- Why trust the text of the Bible, when it's been translated and copied countless times?

- What about science and Christianity?

- What about evolution?

- What about the problem of evil?

- What about other religions?

- What about atrocities committed in the name of Christ?

- What about God's judgment and hell?

Why trust the Bible, when it's been translated and copied countless times?

Many people today believe the scenario expressed by fiction author, Dan Brown, who says the Bible is unreliable because it has "evolved through countless translations, additions and revisions."[46] None of that is true.

Concerning translations, today's Bible scholars translate the text exactly *once*—from Hebrew (Old Testament) or Greek (New Testament) to English. Today's modern translations of the Bible are compiled by committees of scholars working together to compare and accurately translate ancient texts. It would be unthinkable for modern translators to use a recent translation as the basis for a new translation apart from the earliest texts.

The notion that copying a text renders it unknowable is also false. Consider that every well known text we have from antiquity has

---

46   Dan Brown, *The DaVinci Code*, p. 231

been copied, but nobody doubts that the copies reliably reproduce the original. Have you ever read Plato, Homer, or any other ancient author? Were you haunted by the thought that you have no idea whether the text is reliable? Probably not, because copies are fully capable of transmitting the original content. They don't have to be perfect because the meaning still comes across.

Many are surprised to learn that our copies of the Bible come from a time much earlier than for any other text from antiquity. For most ancient books, we have no copies closer than five hundred to fifteen hundred years from the time of original writing. With the New Testament, we have pieces from within twenty five years of the original and whole manuscripts not much later. Also, the ancient copies number in the thousands—by far more than any other ancient text. Comparing these gives scholars a high level of confidence that we have an accurate text.

For the Old Testament, the gap between the last book and our earliest manuscripts used to be fourteen hundred years. Then, when the Dead Sea Scrolls surfaced, it went down to only a couple hundred years. The Scrolls also confirmed that later manuscripts had been transmitted with a good level of accuracy.

After enlightenment scholars launched two centuries of attack on the integrity of the biblical text, more recent text discoveries have confirmed the accuracy of the Bible from cover to cover.

What about science and the Bible?

Many people believe that faith in the Bible is incompatible with science. I would argue to the contrary that today one can be a consistent scientific thinker and a committed believer in Jesus Christ and the Bible. Although the church has resisted the advance of science at various points in history, I believe nothing in the Bible necessarily contradicts any area of scientific consensus.

We should note first that the Bible's worldview is in harmony with the first principles of science in that both believe in the uniformity of cause and effect in a real material world. This is different from most religions where natural events are caused by spirits. It's also different than the eastern mystical view that the material world is not actually real. You would have to abandon either of these beginning points in order to be a scientist.

No religious worldview is as harmonious with science as Christianity. Most philosophers of science agree: It's no accident that modern science arose in Christian-influenced Europe. All the early scientists, like Galileo, Copernicus, Kepler, and Newton were strong theists. They believed it made sense to look for reason in nature because a rational God created it. Only much later, during the enlightenment in Europe, did the view arise that science and spiritual matters were in contradiction.

The biblical worldview holds that, while cause and effect are real and account for most events, there is also the real possibility of direct divine intervention at any given time. Therefore, Christians can accept scientific explanations for natural events while also accepting biblical explanations for supernatural events.

Biblical teaching doesn't contradict science, but it does contradict "scientism." Scientism is the view that scientific observation and explanations of the material world must always be non-supernatural. In scientism, one may never invoke God to explain anything. Natural explanations are the only valid forms of knowledge. Everything else is unknowable opinion and interpretation. Science, a common sense way to study the world, has accomplished a lot during its history. Scientism, a naked philosophical assumption, devoid of backing, has never accomplished anything. It only limits and censors any and every view that refers to observations or explanations involving the non-material, whether it's God or even our own minds.

Evolution

Earlier in the book, we saw that the origin of life would only have been possible through intentional design. To date, no one has advanced any plausible alternative explanation, including evolution (since the mechanism of Darwinian evolution requires already self-replicating organisms). Once life was created, the process of mutation and natural selection could come into play. Most Christians believe that natural history involves a combination of divine intervention and natural processes, including natural selection, or evolution.

We don't know how much of life's development is the result of divine intervention, and how much evolved naturally. Depending on how one interprets Genesis, a wide range of scenarios is possible.

Some Christians go as far as believing in theistic evolution—an evolutionary process directed at points by God. I personally don't think this is a likely explanation, because it doesn't accord well with the language of Genesis 1. Perhaps God created only a limited number of "kinds," or general categories of creatures, and a process of natural selection has caused the variety we see today. Perhaps these categories were not all created at the same time, but were gradually introduced over many years. Bible scholars have shown several ways to see this in the text of Genesis.[47] Still others argue that the creation in Genesis is actually a re-creation of a world that already existed but had been substantially destroyed.[48]

All biblical believers agree on one point: the human race was a product of direct divine intervention, not merely natural process. This point must be true if people have souls or spirits. Obviously, no process of biological evolution could ever produce a spirit that would survive the death of the body. Belief in a conscious afterlife is nonsense unless we acknowledge a nonbiological, nonmaterial

---

47 See Francis Schaeffer, *Genesis in Space and Time,* (Downers Grove IL: IVP Books, 1972) or James Porter Moreland, John Mark Reynolds, John J. Davis, Howard J. Van Till, Paul Nelson, and Robert C. Newman, *Three Views of Creation and Evolution,* (Grand Rapids MI: Zondervan, 1999).

48 This view is called the "gap theory" because it sees a gap between Genesis 1:1 "In the beginning, God created the heavens and the earth," and verse 2, "and the earth became formless and void." Notice this reading accepts the marginal "became" (NIV) rather than "was." Under this view, most of natural history happened before verse 2. The earth becoming a wasteland could refer to some more recent event, and the rest of the chapter tells how God re-created many populations, including humans.

dimension to humans. This nonmaterial soul or spirit could only derive from a nonmaterial source—God himself. The Bible explicitly teaches this in Genesis 2:7 and elsewhere. Of course, science can not answer the question of whether humans have a spirit by using material metrics.

So special creation must have happened as we saw in earlier chapters, and specific creative interventions were probably combined with periods of evolution. Nothing science has learned contradicts this picture.

What about the problem of evil?

Why would a good God create a world like ours, so full of evil and injustice? Many think this is the most important objection to the biblical picture of God. Simply stated, if the Creator of the world is good and all-powerful, why is his creation so often bad? Is it because he doesn't want to prevent evil? Then he must not be good. Or is it that he cannot prevent evil? Then he must not be all-powerful.

In responding to the problem of evil, remember: this is not just a problem for theists. Non-theists have huge problems in this area. They can't even explain what evil is, and based on their assumptions, should see nothing wrong with the way our world is. What is, is right under naturalism, so this is no answer at all. Naturalists must embrace evil as inevitable and really pointless like everything else, including good.

Eastern religion holds that people suffer because they deserve it. This highly implausible view holds that even babies that starve to death deserve their fate because of wrongdoing in a previous life.

Animism has no answer for the problem of evil, and in fact doesn't even acknowledge the problem. In animism and polytheism, the gods are evil as well. They lie, they kill, and they commit adultery. So this complex of religions embraces human evil and suffering, viewing the world as exactly the way it should be and always will be.

Against this backdrop, Biblical Christianity stands out as the most satisfying explanation for the ongoing evil in our world.

The fall

The Bible starts with the claim that God built free will into humans at the beginning. Indeed, morally evil deeds are only possible for free choosing beings. If a kid swats another kid with a stick, we don't lecture the stick. The stick was doing what the kid made it do. Only the free moral agent—the kid—would be guilty of wrongdoing. A free choosing being is a personal being. Beings with consciousness are not subject to natural laws for their decisions. They can be truly free.

When God made free choosing beings, he created the *possibility* of evil, but humans delivered the *actuality* of evil when they chose to reject God's leadership. The human fall from God's intended position of closeness and obedience to him resulted in a catastrophic fall for the whole planet. Without God's protection and leadership everything on this planet is out of control. The guilty suffer along with the innocent.

Some argue that God made an immoral decision when he created a world that he knew would result in such trouble. Clearly, God made a decision to create freedom even though he knew it would lead to pain and suffering. So he made a value judgment: freedom was more important than the avoidance of evil. But why should God value freedom so highly?

We don't know the full answer to this last question, but we do know part of the answer.

Personhood

As already mentioned, personhood requires freedom. There can be no personality where there is no free choice. Suppose you built a robot that could speak and then you programmed it to say "I love you," when you push a button. You push the button several times when you get home from work, but you feel no pleasure from hearing the statement. That's because this statement is not the product of a thinking, choosing person. The robot doesn't love you; it is only repeating what you programmed it to say. You might as well talk to yourself.

This simple illustration shows the importance of freedom. Without freedom, there would be no personality other than God. When we say "free choice," we mean truly free, not just free in word only. If God created any freedom, it must be possible to misuse that freedom.[49]

Some atheistic authors have claimed that God should have created people with freedom who would always choose to do good. But this is a nonsense statement, just like saying that God should have created a square triangle. Any effort to describe freedom that has only one choice is an exercise in absurdity. Therefore, we see the trade-off between two desirable things: on one hand, personality, and on the other, an evil-free universe. God has rejected the second alternative of programmed machines in favor of beings with personalities like his own.

Why so long?

Perhaps God had reasons for risking evil. But why, after people chose evil, didn't God put an end to the problem and start over? This option seems reasonable enough, but upon more reflection, we realize it would be a simplistic and dangerous solution.

First, we need to realize that revolution—the rejection of divine leadership—is based on suspicion of God's character. In Genesis, for instance, Satan told Eve that the real reason God forbade them to

---

49 True freedom need not imply *complete* freedom. The original humans had complete freedom to do anything within their ability. But that freedom was diminished significantly at the time of the fall. Humans have lost the freedom to turn toward God, and now it requires a special work of the Holy Spirit to draw people toward Christ to the point where their will becomes free again (John 6:44; 12:32; Romans 5:12-21). We also lose freedom of choice when we become addicts, or when others' choices negatively impact us. Even with these impediments, humans remain free enough in their choices to be responsible.

eat certain fruit was that he was unwilling to let humans become like himself (Genesis 3:5). This shows that Satan brings accusations against the character of God, charging that he is not loving and that he is holding out on his creatures and repressing them. Satan must have made similar claims to the host of other creatures that inhabit the universe, because we know that some of them also joined his revolution (Revelation 12:3-4, 7, 9).

What would it look like to the citizens of the universe if every time someone revolted, God immediately zapped them out of existence? Then, he could look around at the other creatures and ask, "Are there any other questions?" Wouldn't this tend to confirm that God is unloving and self-serving? Clearly, the simple solution is not as workable as it seems. It would probably be only a matter of time before another revolt occurred, followed by another purge. This might continue throughout the course of eternity.

God's alternative

God decided to deal with the problem of the misuse of freedom once and for all. Instead of immediately terminating the revolution, he let it develop fully. Today, through the futility of human history and through Jesus' self-sacrificial intervention at the cross, evidence is accumulating that will render revolution implausible in the future. God has delayed forceful intervention in our history so that evil can be taken out of the way once and for all, rather than in an endless series of revolts and judgments (Hebrews 9:12, 26, 28; 10:10).

Viewed this way, the value judgment God made must be justified in the larger picture. We don't know what the full picture is, but we can see how it might explain why God didn't put an immediate end to evil. According to the Bible, God will eventually put an end to the revolt. This happens when Jesus returns to take over the world again for God. In the meantime, Paul said his job was:

> To make plain to everyone the administration of this mystery, which for ages past was kept hidden in God, who created all

things. His intent was that now, through the church, the manifold wisdom of God should be made known to the rulers and authorities in the heavenly realms, according to his eternal purpose which he accomplished in Christ Jesus our Lord. (Ephesians 3:9-11)[50]

Is it fair?

Why should Adam's decision still affect us today? Wouldn't it be fair to let each of us make our own decision?

To answer this, we have to come to grips with the power of free choice. If someone decided to hold you up on the way home and then shot you, that guy's choices would affect you powerfully. Yes, it's unfair. But that's the way freedom works. Anything can happen. What would be the alternative? If God only allowed those choices that don't adversely affect anyone else, there would be virtually no freedom at all. Free people can choose to be unfair and to harm other people.

People sometimes feel angry about this, but where do we think God should draw the line? He decided to allow humans to do as they wish, including rejecting his leadership. This level of freedom was a

---

50 The mention of secrecy in verse 9 is interesting, but unfortunately the reason for secrecy lies outside the scope of this book. Suffice it to say that God apparently dept his purpose secret until the last minute, as part of his strategic plan of war with Satan. This desire for secrecy actually led to the biggest mistake Satan ever made—conspiring to kill Christ.

We would argue that the master rebel did not realize this was exactly what Christ wanted (1 Corinthians 2:8). God created confusion and secrecy by deliberately omitting to mention in the Old Testament prophecies that there would be two comings of King Messiah. Also, this need for secrecy explains why passages we studied earlier, like the servant songs in Isaiah, do not come out and say they refer to the Messiah.

God set up the predictive material in such a way that, up until the minute Jesus died, it was hard to say whom these predictions referred to. But one minute after Christ's death, it was impossible to deny the clear fulfillment! See also Luke 24:44-48; John 12:32-34; 16:25; Romans 16:25; 1 Peter 1:12. See a full explanation in Dennis McCallum, *Satan and His Kingdom: What the Bible Says and How It Matters to You*, Ch. 4-5.

high level indeed, and, to God, having such freedom was better than avoiding the possibility of evil.

The upshot of this scenario is that we cannot expect fairness in a fallen world. The world would be fair and benign if God were in direct control of it, as he will be when Christ returns. In the meantime, we are alienated from God to a terrible degree. "The whole creation has been groaning as in the pains of childbirth," as it waits the day when "the creation itself will be liberated from its bondage to decay and brought into the glorious freedom of the children of God" (Romans 8:21-22).

Under the biblical worldview, we believe in what Francis Schaeffer called "the uniformity of cause and effect in an open system."[51] That means that most things we see in the world are simply the result of cause and effect, as science also argues. However, since the system is open, not closed, God can also intervene at any time he chooses to alter the cause and effect sequence. This is why we pray.

This is also why it is usually a mistake to attribute illness and death to the wrath of God. Jesus taught this when he said the people killed by the collapse of a tower in his day were no different than anyone else. Why, then, did they die? Because they were standing under the tower when it fell (See Luke 13:1-5). Jesus resisted the rabbinic theology that attributed illness, poverty, and misfortune to the justice of God. Even though there are times when God may judge people through calamity in this life (Isaiah 45:7), this is not the norm. Wicked people often prosper more than the righteous, and innocent babies suffer. The Christian thinker realizes these events are the result of the general fallen status of the world.

God permissively allows cause and effect to carry on, waiting for a time when he will take control of the situation. In the meantime, he will intervene in life periodically on his own initiative and will intervene even more often when invited to do so by one of us in prayer (James 4:2; 5:16).

---

51 Explained in Francis Schaeffer, *The God Who Is There* (Downers Grove IL: IVP Books, 1998) Ch. 2.

The biblical view of cause and effect is much more believable than systems of thought that try to explain everything on the basis of divine action. These other systems try to explain why everything that happens is really fair after all, when it clearly isn't. Biblical teaching, on the other hand, agrees with the findings of modern science that natural cause and effect adequately explain most of what we see. At the same time, we differ from scientism in holding that God can, and does, intervene at times.[52]

What about other religions?

Many of us love people who belong to different religions, and in any case, we feel uncomfortable claiming we know the truth while others are mistaken. This leads many to adopt a position that accepts all religions as valid. "Why can't other religions be different paths to the same summit?" Or "all religions teach the same basic principles." These are the cries of someone who is trying to be tolerant and accepting of others' beliefs.

But before you jump on this bandwagon, ask yourself, are we really climbing a mountain here, or are we trying to discover what is true? What if you had some friends who believed cult leader David Koresh was Christ? Knowing what we know now, after his followers burned to death in Texas, isn't it true that his followers were deceived by a false messiah? How about the followers of Jim Jones, the poisoner of Guyana? Today we can say without flinching that these sincere, convinced followers were sadly mistaken. How much better it would have been to convince them they were mistaken before it was too late!

When you think about it, a lot of people must be mistaken about religion. When the Hindu scriptures teach that souls are reincarnated,

---

52 People argue that God failing to intervene when he could makes him responsible for evil. But causing evil and not preventing it are not the same. Yes, in one sense, everything that happens is within the permissive will of God, because he has allowed the situation to develop. But scripture is clear that God's moral will is constantly being violated (Matthew 23:37; 2 Peter 3:9).

and Christianity teaches that "man is destined to die once, and after that to face judgment" (Hebrews 9:27), someone has to be wrong. Of course, they could both be wrong (if there is no afterlife), but they *cannot* both be right.

This turns out to be the case in one area after another. The religions of the world contradict each other directly; they do *not* teach basically the same thing. This is true whether they are teaching on the nature of God, the nature of man, the way of salvation, or the meaning of history. These differences are particularly sharp when we compare the religions of the world to biblical Christianity. World religions share many similarities to one another, but very few with Jesus' teaching. We have to decide which we think is right.

Such a search will turn up some interesting facts.

First of all, many religious scriptures appear to be based on speculation about nature. Another important source for sacred writings, in some cases, is the cultural background of the author(s).

For instance, an Egyptian religious myth that seems to be speculation teaches how clouds are created. According to this myth, the god Apsu masturbates and his semen issues in clouds. Such a myth draws most of its insight from nature: the speculator has seen clouds rain on the fields, and the resulting fertility is one of the most commonly worshiped features of nature.[53] The idea seems to be that, just as man's semen fertilizes the woman, the semen of the clouds brings fertility to the fields. The earth is often pictured as a mother and the bride of the sky for this reason. Today we know that clouds are not created in this way and there are other reasons why fields are fertile.[54]

How should the honest thinker today respond to such a myth?

---

53 This myth is from an inscription inside the pyramids of Mernere and Pepi II, dating from about the twenty-fourth century B.C. Available in translation by Phyllis Ackerman, "The Dawn of Religions," Vergilius Ferm, *Forgotten Religions* (New York: The Philosophical Library, 1950).

54 "The divine couple, Heaven and Earth... are one of the *leitmotiven* [central motifs] of universal mythology." Mircea Eliade, *Patterns in Comparative Religion*, 240. See his whole discussion on "Earth, Woman, Fertility," 239-264. See many other examples of earth mother cults in James G. Frazer, , 39-42.

The answer is clear. Even if we had a relative or loved one who believed it, it simply is not true. By admitting this, you're not rejecting those who believe in false worldviews. Disagreeing about what is true doesn't mean you would assume a sense of superiority over others. In fact, Jesus calls on us to love those who are not Christians just as we love those who are (Matthew 5:46-47).

Also, we can study religion to understand the meaning and value to those who believe it. Even if these religions bring comfort and joy to those who hold them, we dare not overlook the issue of truth. When we say God is real and his word is true, we are not merely suggesting that these are true for us, or true in some religious sense. We are saying God is as real as we are, and that his word is true whether we believe it or not.

Once we begin to admit that some religious teachings are false (like the bizarre one mentioned above), we have to wonder where the line should be drawn. Should only the worst religions be rejected, such as those promoting human sacrifice or cannibalism?[55] Or should we also reject those teaching that women cannot enter the eternal state (Hinduism)?[56] We quickly realize that once we are prepared to say any religion is wrong, we have crossed the threshold into a critical assessment of all religion. We have admitted that all paths might not lead to God.

A critical approach to religion has a positive side, too. When a view is falsifiable, it is also believable. Any claim that is not falsifiable cannot be discussed rationally. For instance, consider the claim

---

55 Eliade, one of the most well-known comparative religion scholars in recent times, takes relativism to its logical extreme when he says, "It should always be remembered, before passing judgment upon cannibalism, that it was founded by divine Beings." And, "Before pronouncing a moral judgment upon these customs, one should remember this—that to kill a man, and eat him or preserve his head as a trophy, is to imitate the behavior of the Spirits, or of the gods. Thus, replaced in its own context, the act is a religious one, a ritual." Mircea Eliade, *Myths, Dreams and Mysteries: The Encounter Between Contemporary Faiths and Archaic Realities,* (NY: Harper & Row, 1967) 47, 200. Are we seriously ready to take the denial of objective truth this far? If not, where do we draw the line?

56 Denise L. Carmody and John T. Carmody, *Ways to the Center* (Belmont, Calif.: Wadsworth Publishing Co., 1984), p. 89.

that UFOs exist but they only appear when no one is watching. Such a claim can be neither verified nor falsified. It is, therefore, beyond discussion because it depends on blind faith. The realm of blind faith is also the realm of mindless faith, as we saw earlier with the story of taking unknown pills your friend offers to make you well.

On the other hand, no sophisticated view can be verified on every point. Even the most rigorous scientific outlook has to accept first principles based on implication and faith, such as the belief that our world is real and that our senses convey truth. Yet this doesn't mean a scientific worldview is unfalsifiable in general. Some areas are falsifiable, and others are not.

This is also the case in religion and religious scriptures. Although we may be unable to verify or falsify some areas, other areas can be checked. If the areas we can check prove false, we have no reason to believe the areas we cannot check. This is why we should reject any scripture's claims to truth if they contain verifiable, gross errors—and this is bad news for most religions. So too, why accept the truth claims of any religion or scripture if it offers no reason for belief? Again, we see the amazing difference where the Bible is concerned. The powerful evidence we went over earlier is missing from other religious texts.

To summarize, it seems clear that some religious claims are false. If this is true with some, then it may be true with others in whole or in part. Therefore, we should try to evaluate religious teaching, not only from the standpoint of the good feelings they create in their followers, but also from the standpoint of whether they are true. When religions contradict each other, we should not claim both are true.

If you conclude that one religious doctrine or sacred scripture is more believable that need not imply personal arrogance or intolerance toward others. We make evaluations of this kind in other areas of life every day. If you are unable to evaluate some teachings at your present level of knowledge, you could always remain neutral on those questions. But that's quite different from saying that two contradictory statements are both true.

So the real question is not whether people adhere to religious views because their families did, or whether they may find comfort in that. The deeper question is whether any of these are actually true, in the sense of being real. Regarding the view that people believe whatever they were raised to believe, we can only observe that this view is in error. Today, for instance, Christianity is expanding rapidly with thousands of converts weekly in lands that have no history of Christian belief, like India and China. Meanwhile, in the west, where Christianity has traditionally held sway, belief in Christ is in free-fall.

The Bible teaches that Jesus is the only time when God put on humanity. He is also the only provision for forgiving sin. His death alone can forgive our debt to a holy God. He himself said, "I am the way, the truth, and the life. Nobody comes to the Father but through me" (John 14:6). He also said, "All who came before me were robbers and thieves" (John 10:8). He warned that powerful forces of deception seek to lead people astray (John 8:44). He said of Satan, "The thief comes only to steal and kill and destroy; I came that they may have life, and have it abundantly" (John 10:10).

So according to Jesus, we live in a world where people are being led astray and are in daily danger because of his bitter enemy. We should all consider carefully the dangers of discounting Jesus after he was so powerfully validated by God. According to Jesus, the idea that all religions are the same, or okay, is wrong. We have to decide what to believe.

What about atrocities committed in the name of Jesus?

The church has done some great things in its history, and many vital, healthy churches today meet the needs of their own people as well as serving the poor around the world. However, modern Christians have some questions to answer about problems in the history of the church.

In fact, the history of the "Christian church" has been quite disappointing from a biblical point of view. Examples of atrocities committed in the name of Jesus abound, and people could reasonably throw these up as a falsification of Jesus' teaching. For instance, through much of Christian history, opponents of the church were subjected to torture and cruel death.[57] Then there were the religious wars, including the Crusades, resulting in hundreds of thousands of deaths under the banner of the Cross (often to the sound of hymns of thanksgiving).[58]

Praises to God also accompanied genocidal massacres of entire Jewish communities long before Hitler.[59] During Hitler's time, much

---

57 During the Inquisition, torture of children and the aged was to be kept light, but only pregnant women were exempt, and then only until after delivery. Death at the burning stake for heretics was carried out by the secular authorities because "the church could not shed blood." Ronald Finucane, "Persecution and Inquisition," *Eerdmans' Handbook to the History of Christianity* (Grand Rapids, MI: Eerdmans, 1977) 31. This entire section (pp. 34-323) is an excellent and fair explanation of the problem of persecution during this period.

58 After marching around Jerusalem "barefoot, singing penitential hymns," the crusaders broke into the city. "There followed a horrible bloodbath. All the defenders were killed as well as many civilians. Women were raped, and infants thrown against walls. Many of the city's Jews had taken refuge in the synagogue, and the crusaders set fire to the building with them inside. According to an eyewitness, at the Porch of Solomon horses waded in blood." Justo L. Gonzalez, *The Story of Christianity,* Vol. 1 (New York: Harper & Row, 1984) 1, 295-296.

59 For an excellent but heart rending collection of source readings in translation from this period (many written by church officials), see Jacob R. Marcus, ed., *The Jew in the Medieval World,* (Antheneum, N.Y.: Antheneum, 1969), 155-158. A striking incident of church persecution involved the Jews of Passau. Under torture they admitted that they had obtained several hosts (communion wafers) and "that when they had stabbed the hosts, blood flowed from them; that the form of a child arose; and that when they tried to burn the wafers in an oven two angels and two doves appeared." Four of the arrested Jews converted to Christianity and were treated kindly as a result: they were merely beheaded. The rest were torn with hot pincers and burned alive. Examples of such atrocities abound in the history of the church. Marcus includes a score of typical examples, such as the burning of over two thousand Jewish men, women, and children in Strasbourg in 1349 (p. 45). These examples are included because some church members today have difficulty admitting the reality of church-caused atrocities. Note that the accounts mentioned here were not written by enemies of the church, but are original accounts written by clergymen at the time and correlated with parallel accounts.

of the German Lutheran church, the Roman Catholic Church, and even some American churches supported his regime.[60] How could such events happen if Christianity is a faith based on truth and love?

To understand this, we need to look at the development of certain trends in church history that eventually took much of the church far away from what God intended it to be.

The early period

Early church leaders, fearing heresy, began to carefully control people's access to the Bible. They argued that only church leaders were competent to interpret scripture.[61] In addition, the pressure of persecution tended to foster legalism, hyper-strictness, and anti-Semitism.

Later in the 300s, when Christianity was embraced by the Roman government, money and power began to flow into the church. The faith described in the Bible was increasingly distorted by the addition of popular superstition. Sometimes confused or corrupt leaders even replaced the biblical message completely with a message more suitable for attaining control of the situation.

---

60   For example, at the time of the Weimar republic, "It is estimated that seventy to eighty percent of the Protestant pastors allied themselves with... the *Deutschnational Volkspartei*. This party advocated "every expression of justifiable anti-Semitism." David Rausch, *Legacy of Hatred: Why Christians Should Not Forget the Holocaust* (Chicago: Moody Bible Institute, 1984), 50-51. For their part, the Catholic church concluded a Concordat (or treaty of friendship) with Hitler. ("Concordat between the Holy See and the German Reich [with Supplementary Protocol and Secret Supplement]" July 20, 1933 available at http://www.concordatwatch.eu).

61   This remarkably early (about 110 AD?) development can be seen in Ignatius of Antioch (unless, as some scholars think, these passages are forgeries from two centuries later). He argues, "Let no man do anything connected with the Church without the bishop," and, "He who does anything without the knowledge of the bishop does [in reality] serve the devil." That the pressure of heresy was the driving force behind this restrictive new teaching is evident in this passage and in the letter to the Philadelphians: "Keep yourselves from those evil plants which Jesus Christ does not tend [heretics].... For as many as are of God and of Jesus Christ are also with the bishop." Ignatius of Antioch, "Letter to the Smyrnaeans," "Letter to the Trallians," and "Letter to the Philadelphians," in Alexander Roberts and James Donaldson, eds., *The Ante-Nicene Fathers, Vol. 1,* (Grand Rapids, Mich.: Eerdmans, 1985), 66, 80, 89, 90.

One of the earliest misfortunes in church history was the abandonment of the grammatical-historical method of interpreting the Bible.[62] Instead, the narratives were converted into allegories with symbolic meaning. This left the interpreter free to assign his own interpretation to the text.[63] Since anyone could assign his own meaning, the Bible tended to lose authority. Instead, church leaders claimed the authority to determine which allegory was appropriate in each case.

Under this regimen, people gradually began to relate more to icons (holy pictures and statues) and temples than they did to the written Word. The church excused this change by pointing out that the people were illiterate and that it would be divisive to allow each person to reach his own conclusion about Scripture's meaning. But this was not really a sufficient answer, because oral societies are able to learn and study the written Scriptures through public reading (1 Timothy 4:13). Besides, the church should have taken an interest in teaching more people to read. Later, during the Protestant Reformation, it was the church that pushed for universal compulsory education so people could read the Bible.[64]

---

62 A grammatical-historical interpretive method seeks the meaning using the rules of grammar in the original language, colored as appropriate by the historical context. It allows for figures of speech and idiomatic expression. Symbolism is only accepted when the text clearly intends to be symbolic. The advent of allegorical interpretation coincided with the intrusion of Platonic philosophy into the thinking of the church. It also stemmed from a desire to present the Old Testament as a Christian book. See a fair but critical treatment in Bernard Ramm, *Protestant Biblical Interpretation* (Grand Rapids, Mich.: Baker, 1970), 23-45. Clement of Alexandria is credited with popularizing the allegorical approach to the Bible and for incorporating Greek philosophy into Christian theology. See his explanation in "The Stromata," *The Ante-Nicene Fathers,* Vol. 1, 322ff. Learn about the grammatical-historical method of interpretation in Roy B. Zuck, *Basic Bible Interpretation* (Wheaton, Ill., Victor Books, 1991).

63 For instance, the church taught that the two swords found by Peter in Luke 22:38 stood for the two authorities established by God over human society. One sword was the civil government (based on the passage in Romans 13:4), and the other was the ecclesiastical (church) authority! On this basis, it became plausible for the church to use armed force against its enemies, as was done in the Crusades and in the many executions of dissenters in Europe over hundreds of years. Geoffrey Bromiley, "The Interpretation of the Bible," Frank E. Gabelein, ed., *The Expositor's Bible Commentary* (Grand Rapids, Mich.: Zondervan, 1978), 69.

64 Both Luther and Calvin "believed that it was important for all Christians to read the

The outcome

Once the Bible was taken out of the hands of the average person, no one could prevent teachings alien to the Bible from entering the church. Eventually the church began to openly claim that it could generate new divinely inspired material apart from any biblical authority. Church leaders became so powerful that they eventually made opposition to the church a capital crime in Europe. Hundreds of thousands of religious dissidents (including Jews) were tortured and killed in Europe during the medieval period.[65]

Modern readers find it hard to understand how such disparity between the church teaching and the Bible (upon which it was supposedly based) ever came to pass. But once biblical authority was subjected to human authority, anything could happen. Although the Protestant movement in the 1500s corrected many of these excesses, the Reformed, Lutheran, and Anglican churches continued to practice the power tactics of their predecessors. Dissenters and Jews were persecuted and killed in the name of God.[66]

Responding to abuses

Today, some churches are still openly evil, as when they teach race hatred and group suicide, or when they bilk money from the ignorant for greedy church leaders. Others are merely ridiculous, as when they engage in superstitious practices or various extra-biblical types

Bible. They urged the state to help establish an educational system." Merle L. Borrowman, "Education," *The Academic American Encyclopedia*, Vol. 7, 60-61.

65   See source reading in translation relating to this power struggle in Brian Teirney, *The Crisis of Church and State: 1050-1300* (Englewood Cliffs, N.J.: Prentice-Hall, Inc., 1964). The three-hundred-year history of the Inquisition can be studied in any survey of church or medieval history.

66   According to Gonzales, the persecution of Anabaptists, carried out by both Protestants and Catholics, involved more fatalities than the famous Roman persecution of Christians during the first two centuries of Christianity. Yet while everyone knows about the early persecution of Christians, this merciless persecution of the Anabaptists is virtually unknown to laymen today. Justo L. Gonzales, *The Story of Christianity*, Vol. 2 (New York: Harper & Row, 1984), 56.

of ritualism, like snake handling. Of course, other churches are completely innocent of such abuses.

Why would God allow the church to go so far astray, and how can we speak of Christianity without also speaking of the church? Is it really possible to divorce the biblical message from the historical church?

The answers to these questions can be found in the Bible itself. Jesus predicted that many impostors would invade the church:

> Watch out for false prophets. They come to you in sheep's clothing, but inwardly they are ferocious wolves. By their fruit you will recognize them. Do people pick grapes from thornbushes, or figs from thistles? Likewise every good tree bears good fruit, but a bad tree bears bad fruit.... Thus, by their fruit you will recognize them. Not everyone who says to me, "Lord, Lord," will enter the kingdom of heaven. (Matthew 7:15-17, 20-21)

In this passage, Jesus teaches that we cannot trust professed Christian leaders based merely on their word. We have to evaluate any leader's truthfulness by examining that person's morality ("fruit") and faithfulness to the biblical message.[67] In cases where church leaders are involved in violence, lying, or immorality, they have obviously failed this test. Under the biblical picture, where a great deceiving enemy (Satan) is fighting against the people of God, it becomes less surprising that people are fooled into thinking they are following God when they are not.

Observe in the passage cited above that Jesus puts the burden on the individual believer to distinguish the true teachers from the false. This means we will never reach a point where we can safely say, "I let my priest or pastor figure out what is right in theological

---

67 Compare Deuteronomy 13:1-5; and 2 Timothy 3:13. The peril of false prophecy has always been present, and it has always been the responsibility of the individual to discern it.

matters." Paul also warned Timothy that fidelity to the Bible would be an essential test:

> Preach the Word... For the time will come when men will not put up with sound doctrine. Instead, to suit their own desires, they will gather around them a great number of teachers to say what their itching ears want to hear. They will turn their ears away from the truth and turn aside to myths. (2 Timothy 4:2-4)

Notice also that the Bible was not written to theologians or church leaders (with the exception of the Pastoral Epistles), but to the common people in local fellowships. Even if a group was illiterate, Paul ordered that his letters be read to "all the brothers" (1 Thessalonians 5:27).[68] So, although we should listen to the scholarship of leaders, we should never shirk our responsibility to interpret and apply the Bible, discerning false teachers when we hear them. Indeed, how could it be otherwise? If God protected us from all deception, he would have to completely disrupt the freedom of the human race.

In the final analysis, we need to make a clear distinction between the teachings of the Bible and the practices of those counterfeiting truth. Deception is real, and the enemy of human souls will infiltrate and distort the truth as much as possible.

We should not forget the important exceptions to the lamentable trend in the church through history. Christians have contributed to, and led, a number of important social changes. For example, most historians see the Christian church as central (though tardy) in the abolition of human slavery. Universal education is a legacy of the Reformation. In many countries, the only hospitals and schools in existence were put there by Christians. Unfortunately, the good deeds

---

68 See also Hebrews 13:22, 24, where the author says, "Brothers, I urge you to bear with my word of exhortation.... Greet all your leaders and all God's people." So the book was not addressed to leaders, but to the other members of the church. Also, Colossians 3:16 says, "Let the word of Christ dwell in you richly as you teach and admonish one another with all wisdom."

of some churches cannot blot out the horrific record put up in the name of Jesus.

Regardless of how people may have misused the truths in the Bible, the Bible says that when we come before God, we will answer to the standard of truth (Romans 2:2). So we are accountable to biblical teaching, not to strange church groups that grew up over the years. Church tradition is a human product, subject to all the fallibility of humans. Only God's word is reliable.

What about judgment and hell?

According to the Bible, God is 'just.' In other words, he is not able to accept evil passively without eventually doing something about it. His reaction to evil is called judgment, and we have come to refer to God's final judgment as "hell."[69]

Hell is a disturbing concept for anyone who thinks seriously about it, because it is not remedial but retributive. In other words, the idea is not to fix people, but to repay them fairly for what they did. You cannot make the concept of hell benign, because it is truly terrible. However, if hell is real, we have to come to grips with it. A few points will help here.

First, the Bible teaches that God gives everyone what theologians call "common grace." Common grace is a gift that enables people to know God is there and that he is the personal Creator of the world.

---

69   The final judgment is hell, but God can also judge in lesser ways before the final judgment. According to the Bible, he can judge people by shortening their mortal lives (as in the case of Sodom and Gomorrah) or order them to be killed (as in the case of the conquest of Canaan). These temporal judgments are fair, because humans lie under a death sentence anyway. From God's point of view, having their physical lives shortened is not the worst thing that can happen to people. All people are destined for physical death even without any additional judgment from God. Children in these scenarios are taken to heaven, so they don't suffer at all. Notice that such judgments are never a license for people to kill unless specifically ordered to do so by God. See the thinking in Deuteronomy 9:5 "It is not for your righteousness or for the uprightness of your heart that you are going to possess their land, but it is because of the wickedness of these nations that the Lord your God is driving them out before you...." So in these cases, as in the case of hell, the real question is whether God has the right to judge.

The apostle Paul explains:

> What may be known about God is plain to [people], because
> God has made it plain within them. For since the creation
> of the world God's invisible qualities—his eternal power and
> divine nature—have been clearly seen, being understood
> from what has been made, so that men are without excuse.
> (Romans 1:19-20)

This passage teaches that even those who have never heard of the
Bible have access to two sources of insight about God. One is looking
"within" themselves. Jesus also referred to this when he said he would
"draw all men to himself" (John 12:32). In other words, God sees to
it that people know within themselves that they are spiritual beings
and that they need God. We considered this evidence earlier in the
chapter on consciousness.

The other source of insight is "what has been made," which
refers to nature. We already saw why honest reflection on the rest
of nature suggests the presence of a Creator God. On the basis of
these two things, Paul says people are "without excuse." What does
this mean?

Actually, we don't know how God will deal with those who have
not heard the gospel. We do know, however, that under the biblical
view of justice we are responsible for what we know, not for what we
don't know. Thus, infants are apparently always taken to heaven.[70] If
people without the Bible are "without excuse," it must mean they are
able to do something that would result in God applying the death of
Christ to them.

While the Bible doesn't explain the required response, it does rule
out certain possibilities. In verse 25 of the same chapter, it says God
would not accept those who "worshiped and served created things
rather than the Creator." Apparently, everyone knows intuitively that

---

70   Compare Matthew 18:1-6; Luke 12:47-48; 2 Samuel 12:23. No doubt, the same
applies to severely mentally disabled people.

the creator is greater than his creation. The desire to worship nature probably stems from a desire to avoid the true God behind nature.

Unfortunately, we see little evidence that many people are responding to this common grace in areas where the Christian gospel is unknown, although there are some outstanding exceptions.[71] At the same time, it is nice to know God is active in reaching out to all people. The biblical believer has to trust that a fair God will treat people fairly.

Even with the notion of common grace, the main problems with hell remain unresolved. To fairly evaluate the biblical position on hell, we have to consider the alternatives to the biblical view.

Alternative views

The idea of hell is dreadful. But what is the alternative?

According to the atheistic worldview, there is no afterlife at all, so the question is moot. To the atheist, everyone—evil people and the best people as well—share the same fate: oblivion.

The Eastern mystic foresees no better fate. For them, the devotee must try to escape *maya*—the veil of tears, suffering, and illusion (that is, this world)—in an effort to reach *moksha*, *nirvana*, or similar concepts. But it would be a big mistake to connect these ideas of afterlife with our Western concept of heaven. In biblically inspired religions, individuals continue to exist and know who they are in the afterlife. People are able to relate to each other in a personal way in the new heaven and new earth described in the Bible.

But in Eastern mystical religion, this is not the case. According to the Eastern scriptures, the individual is merged with the universal consciousness, and becomes a part of what is called the "All" or "universal emptiness." You, as a distinct person with feelings and thoughts, cease to exist according to this view.[72]

---

71 Don Richardson documents cases where aboriginal peoples already know about almighty creator God in, *Eternity in Their Hearts* (Ventura, Calif.: Regal Books, 1981).

72 "Entrance into [*nirvana*] by any person means the dissolution at death of all the

Therefore, the Eastern monistic concept of "heaven" is similar to what we in the West would call oblivion, on non-existence. The main benefit people gain from entering this final state is that they no longer have to return through reincarnation to the material world of suffering. This prospect is quite depressing, when the best one can expect is to escape the agony of reincarnation and rebirth in *Maya*.

Polytheistic and other theistic teachings agree that a personal heaven exists. This follows quite naturally from the idea that God is personal. On the other hand, these religions almost invariably teach that there is also a hell, so they agree with Christianity on this point as well. The difference is that entrance into heaven is based on belonging to a privileged class of people or on the performance of religious laws, as seen earlier.

So to summarize, none of the other views on what happens after we die has anything positive to offer.

Heaven without hell?

In modern times, some Christian and Jewish theologians have moved toward a view that a personal heaven exists but that no hell exists. This view is called "Universalism," because it teaches that God will save all people. However, the view has a number of serious problems.

First, if there is no judgment, then we will be in heaven along with an unrepentant Hitler. If this happened, it would make you wonder how God could be unconcerned about the difference between good and evil. Under this picture, God treats evil and good alike. The difference between good and evil would be negligible under this view.

Perhaps God doesn't hold people responsible for evil under the Universalist system because they couldn't help themselves. Perhaps God thinks Hitler's upbringing forced him to commit atrocities under

---

elements whose composition makes him the existent entity he now is." E. A. Burtt, ed., *The Teachings of the Compassionate Buddha* (New York: The New American Library, 1955), 112. So too in Taoism; verse 16 of the Tao Te Ching explains that to "touch ultimate emptiness... is to have stature.... Then though you die, you shall not perish." R. B. Blakney, trans., *The Way of Life: Lao Tzu* (New York: The New American Library, 1955), 68.

Universalism. But if that were true, who created that environment? God himself! If people aren't responsible, someone else must be. The only plausible candidate is God.

Why would a Universalist God allow evil to continue? Without the existence of free will and the responsibility that comes with it, it's hard to see the point of simply watching people helplessly suffer. If God is planning to send us all to everlasting reward anyway, why delay further? Why put the world through thousands of years of fallen history? Ironically, under the Universalists view (intended to portray a kinder, gentler deity), God ends up being sadistic.

If, however, we admit free will exists, we cannot deny human responsibility. Neither can we claim that we make the decisions, but God is responsible. We must accept responsibility if our choices are free, because no one is making us do what we do. We cannot separate free choice from responsibility. (On the other hand, as stated earlier, the Bible indicates that God does not hold responsible babies or others who cannot choose.)

This is why God judges. According to the Bible, people are responsible for the situation on earth, both corporately and individually.

Here is another problem with Universalism: no known scripture teaches this idea of a non-judging, personal God. The authority behind this view comes from people's own imagination. The Universalist God is a product of late enlightenment European and American culture, where people preferred authority figures that were amoral, accepting, and nonjudgmental. But is it reasonable to think I could create a new religion with tenets that please me, and then, just because I believe it, it will actually be true? If this were possible, everyone could simply describe a religion they like, and appropriate gods and afterlives would spring into existence as a result! Unless we have evidence outside of ourselves that a certain view is true, we are simply engaging in wishful thinking. This is the case with Universalism.

A crucial question for any reader of the Bible is, "Does God have the right to judge?" According to the Bible, he does have both the right and the responsibility. The universe is finally answerable to justice, and this is something we have to come to grips with.

Setting the right sentence

So what should the penalty for evil be? Those who have experience with prisons discover most prisoners believe they are being treated unfairly. Perhaps some of them are, but it's also a feature of human nature. People tend to think what they do is not very bad and doesn't deserve much punishment. This is probably why we don't let criminals set their own sentences. They might go too soft on themselves.

God doesn't let us set our own sentences either. He assigns the appropriate sentence for guilty people. We are told that at the judgment day, he will justify his choices for all to see. We don't know exactly how this will work, but we do know the consequences of divine judgment will be eternal separation from God.

The really remarkable thing is not that God judges, but that he has undergone his own judgment. Jesus has made it possible for everyone to escape the sentence of hell at his expense. God is going to judge humans. But in his love, he has made it possible to avoid judgment.

Our response

Now we find ourselves in a situation similar to a man who takes an ocean liner from New York to London. In the fog off Greenland, the ship strikes an iceberg and sinks. The man finds himself in the water beginning to freeze to death, when suddenly out of the fog a lifesaver on a rope comes sailing toward him.

If the man looked away and said, "I don't need that, because there is nothing wrong with me," his reaction would be similar to that of the Universalist or the Eastern mystic.

The man might say, "I did nothing to get into this situation, and I refuse to legitimize the situation by admitting I need that lifesaver. I demand to be bodily removed instantly!" Such a response is not unlike that expressed by the atheist who feels too morally outraged by issues like hell or the existence of evil to appreciate what God is offering.

The only sane approach is to gratefully seize what we can understand now (the lifesaver) and seek explanations later for the part we cannot understand.